500

pizzas & flatbreads

500

pizzas & flatbreads

the only pizza and flatbread compendium you'll ever need

Rebecca Baugniet

SELLERS
PUBLISHING

A Quintet Book

Published by Sellers Publishing, Inc.
P.O. Box 818, Portland, Maine 04104
For ordering information:
(800) 625-3386 Toll Free
(207) 772-1225 Fax
Visit our Web site: www.rsvp.com • E-mail: rsp@rsvp.com

ISBN: 978-1-4162-0522-7
Library of Congress Control Number: 2008900987
QTT.PZB

This book was designed and produced by
Quintet Publishing Limited
6 Blundell Street
London N7 9BH
United Kingdom

Project Editor: Marianne Canty
Designer: Roland Codd
Art Director: Sofia Henry
Photographer: Mike McClafferty
Food Stylist: Wendy Lee
Managing Editor: Donna Gregory
Publisher: James Tavendale

10 9 8 7 6 5 4 3 2 1

Manufactured in Singapore by Pica Digital Pte Ltd.
Printed in China by SNP Leefung Printers Ltd.

contents

introduction

Flatbread has existed for as long as humans have been grinding grains, mixing the resulting flour with water, and baking over hot coals. And for almost just as long, people have made these flatbreads more interesting by covering them with other assorted ingredients.

It is the oldest variety of prepared food – one that appears all over the globe, but that takes on different shapes and textures from region to region, depending on what basic ingredients are available in that part of the world. Ancient Greeks called theirs "plakuntos" and covered them with blends of herbs, garlic, and onion. The Aztecs called theirs "tlaxcalli" and made them with maize, which had first been soaked in water mixed with lime to help remove the husks and soften the grain. Many flatbread recipes have survived through the ages and remain close to those original culinary discoveries. They feature flours made from one or more grains – wheat, millet, rye, maize, rice, and buckwheat, to name but a few. They may also be made from grated tubers or root vegetables, such as potatoes, cassava, beets, and turnips. With the advent of the global food market, those living in urban areas and even those removed from the city – with access to the Internet and home delivery – can taste flavors from far-off countries and evoke memories of ancient civilizations in their own home kitchens.

Flatbreads fall into two main categories – those leavened with yeast or another leavening agent, and those that are unleavened. In the category of leavened flatbread, pizza is the one to have become a truly international phenomenon over the past 60 years, although focaccias, pitas, naans, and others have been gaining more widespread popularity. What sets pizza apart from other flatbreads is the use of tomato as the main topping ingredient. This became common practice around Naples in the eighteenth century and rapidly grew in fame throughout Italy. One hundred years later, pizza was brought to the United States by Italian immigrants and began another metamorphosis. Pizzerias began appearing in cities throughout the country and soon different trends in pizza-making started to emerge, with such delicious results as the Chicago deep-dish pizza, thin crust pizzas, and pan pizzas.

In response to these developments, Neapolitan pizza makers formed an association in 1984 to protect the characteristics of the original Neapolitan pizza, imposing specific rules to be obeyed in order for a pizza to qualify as an authentic Neapolitan pizza. The association accepts only Marinara and Margherita Pizzas made entirely by hand — no mixers or rolling pins allowed. They must measure no more than 12 in. (30 cm.) across and be baked in a wood-fired oven for no more than a minute and a half. Fortunately, the "True Neapolitan Pizza Association" will not be inspecting your kitchen, so have fun and experiment with your favorite topping combinations. Whichever recipe you try first, when you take part in this time-honored process, you are sure to enjoy the results.

equipment

If you plan on making pizzas and flatbreads on a regular basis, you may want to invest in a few pieces of equipment that will encourage successful results, such as a baking stone and a pizza peel. However, these items are not essential to the process, and most of the recipes in this book can be made with ordinary kitchen items.

measuring cups & spoons
Baking is an exact science, so correct measuring equipment is essential. Always use calibrated measuring cups and proper measuring spoons. Flour should be spooned into measuring cups for accurate measurements.

mixing bowls & standing mixers
A variety of mixing bowls is essential in the baker's kitchen. You will need a large bowl in which to make the dough and let it rise. A glass 2-quart measuring bowl can be especially useful for measuring how much your dough has risen. Medium and small bowls are useful for preparing fillings and toppings. A standing mixer with a dough hook attachment allows you to perform other tasks in the kitchen while the kneading is occurring.

rolling pins & boards
Pizza purists will insist that pizza dough must be stretched out by hand, but until you have mastered this technique, a rolling pin is a very useful tool. Many models of rolling pin are available, so choose one that suits your needs and which you find comfortable to work with. The preferred model among bakers remains the wooden French rolling pin with tapered ends. However, in a pinch, you can always use an empty wine bottle. A large wooden board is ideal for rolling out pizza dough, but a well-cleaned countertop will also work nicely.

pizza peels, baking stones & tiles

A pizza peel, or paddle, is a flat, smooth, rounded board with a long handle and tapered front edge that facilitates sliding pizza on and off the baking stone or tiles. It is usually made of hardwood, but it can also be found in aluminum. A flat cookie sheet can also be used as a makeshift pizza peel. Baking stones or quarry tiles are used for making pizzas and flatbreads that require a direct burst of heat to achieve a crisp crust, such as thin-crust pizzas, pizza with a Neapolitan crust, and flatbreads such as naan and pita (which are traditionally baked on oven floors or walls). Baking stones are thick, heavy, round or rectangular pieces of natural lead-free clay that mimic the baking conditions of brick-floored wood-burning ovens. Baking stones are placed on the bottom rack of electric ovens and directly on the floor of a gas oven and preheated with the oven. Unglazed quarry tiles may also be used for the same effect. Peels and baking stones are available in various sizes from gourmet specialty stores or online kitchen equipment suppliers.

skillets, baking pans, cookie sheets & parchment paper

Heavy 9-in. (23-cm.) cast-iron skillets can be used for baking pan pizzas, as can 9-in. (23-cm.) cake pans or a large rimmed rectangular cookie sheet. Chicago-style deep-dish pizzas can be made in 9-in. (23-cm.) round cake pans; however, specialty deep-dish pizza pans are available in different sizes from online distributors. Parchment paper is good for lining baking pans, and it is also useful if you are having trouble transferring your pizza dough from the peel to the baking stone. Simply roll the pizza dough directly onto a square of parchment paper for easy transfers.

tortilla & chapatti presses; tavas & warmers

Specialty equipment is available for certain flatbreads, such as tortillas. If you are making a large quantity of tortillas, you may wish to invest in a tortilla press. These are available in aluminum, cast-iron, plastic, and wood. There's even an electric model that presses and bakes the tortilla in one step. Similar to the tortilla press is the chapatti press, made of cast-iron with two stainless steel plates inside. Tavas are the flat, rimless metal skillets used for frying chapattis and rotis. These can also be used for making tortillas and other flatbreads. Neither the tortilla press nor the chapatti press is essential to making these flatbreads, but they do help speed up the process if you're making them in large quantities. If you have a good, flat skillet or griddle, you can use it for a variety of flatbreads. Tortilla warmers are available in terracotta, porcelain, silicone, and woven baskets. They can be used to keep tortillas and other flatbreads warm throughout the meal.

timers

When baking pizzas and flatbreads, timing is crucial. Either use the timer on your oven or invest in an inexpensive, accurate digital timer.

ingredients

While the dough for pizzas and flatbreads requires only a few ingredients – flour, yeast, salt, olive oil, and water – the toppings can be as plain or as exotic, mild, or aromatic as you choose. Try to use the freshest ingredients whenever possible. Organic ingredients that have been produced free of any chemicals or pesticides will always result in the tastiest baked goods.

wheat & other grain flours

Most recipes for the pizzas in this book call for a blend of all-purpose flour and bread flour. Bread flour contains slightly more gluten than all-purpose flour and helps give the crust its crispy quality. Experiment with different blends of flour to find the perfect crust for your tastes. Whole-wheat flour can replace a portion of the all-purpose flour, but it will result in a somewhat rougher texture. Masa harina is the ideal ingredient for making corn tortillas, though fine cornmeal can be used. Certain flatbread recipes in this book call for flours made from other grains, such as barley, buckwheat, rye, and teff. These are becoming easier to find in the organic sections of larger grocery stores, as well as in health food stores.

yeast & other leavening agents

Yeast is a microscopic single-cell organism commonly used as a leavening agent in breads. Baker's yeast is available as regular active dry yeast, quick-rise active dry yeast, and compressed fresh yeast. Quick-rise yeast, as the name implies, shortens the time it takes to leaven the dough, but is sometimes criticized by bakers who believe that bread and pizza dough requires a longer rising time to achieve the best flavor and texture. Fresh compressed yeast must be refrigerated and used within two weeks. A basic rule for yeast substitutions is 1 envelope of active dry yeast equals 2 1/4 teaspoons of quick-rise yeast or 1 cake of compressed yeast. To "proof" yeast, or test whether it is still alive, dissolve it in warm water, adding a pinch of sugar, and set aside 5 to 10 minutes. If it begins to swell and foam, then it is alive and will act as a leavening agent. Baking powder and baking soda are used as leavening agents in some flatbreads and are commonly available in supermarkets.

oil

Extra-virgin olive oil is used in all recipes unless otherwise specified. Italians add crushed red pepper flakes to olive oil to make "olio santo," which is drizzled in a clockwise motion over a pizza fresh out of the oven.

water

High levels of chlorine and some minerals found in some tap water can have an impact on the action of the yeast in dough. If you are having difficulty with yeast that you are sure is viable, switch to bottled or purified water. In the recipes "warm" water indicates water between 105°F and 115°F (40–45°C). Water that is too cold will not activate yeast, while water that is too hot will kill it. "Tepid" water indicates water at room temperature.

herbs, spices & seeds

Fresh herbs will guarantee the most flavorful sauces and toppings, but dried herbs are an acceptable substitute. A basic rule for herb substitutions is 1 teaspoon chopped fresh herbs equals 1/4 teaspoon of dried and crumbled herbs. Italian herbs such as basil, oregano, and flat-leaf parsley, are all frequently used in pizzas and calzones, so you will want to have them on hand. A wide variety of spices and seeds are used in flatbreads—sesame, poppy, caraway, and flax seeds, which are all widely available in grocery stores. Check health food stores and specialty spice stores for more obscure seeds.

tomatoes & vegetables

Tomatoes grown in the San Marzano region of Italy are the variety preferred by most pizza makers. Check the the labels on canned tomatoes to make sure they are indeed a product of Italy. If they are not available in your area, try out different brands of canned tomatoes to find the ones with the best flavor. Use canned whole tomatoes, as seeds that have been crushed during processing add bitterness to the flavor. If you are using canned chopped tomatoes, you may want to add a bit of sugar to reduce the bitterness. Start with 1/4 teaspoon sugar and add more to taste. If making sauce from fresh tomatoes, opt for vine-ripened ones with a good, strong tomato aroma. Always use the freshest produce you can find. Patronizing local farmers for seasonal produce will guarantee the best flavor as well as being environmentally responsible.

cheeses, sausage & cured meats

Pizzas are the ultimate showcases for all the best Italian cheeses. If you live near a good cheese store, you will have no trouble acquiring authentic mozzarella, ricotta, Parmesan, Asiago, Taleggio, fontina, and provolone. Otherwise, online distributors usually offer overnight delivery. The recipes in this book call for shredded mozzarella — this refers to the block mozzarella available in supermarkets and made popular on American pan pizzas. Fresh mozzarella is the more authentic Italian cheese of choice; it is referred to as bocconcini. It should be used in slices or in torn pieces. Do not limit yourself to Italian cheeses, however, as other cheeses also make luscious toppings for pizzas and flatbread. Chèvre, Boursin, St. Agur, and Gorgonzola are all used with spectacular results in this book. Sausage, removed from its casings and crumbled, is often used as a topping or in sauces. Use a good quality Italian sausage, or one that better suits your tastes. Cured meats such as pancetta, prosciutto, mortadella, and salami are all widely available at supermarket deli counters or Italian deli stores.

store-bought pizza dough & crusts

When you are craving pizza but haven't got the time to make your own dough, store-bought pizza dough is a fine alternative. Good-quality prepared pizza dough is sold both frozen and pre-cooked. Find one that best suits your tastes, or try out other pre-made flatbreads, such as pita or naan, as a base for your homemade pizza. English muffins are the perfect size for children's mini pizzas — top with pizza sauce and some grated cheese and bake in the toaster oven until the cheese has melted for an almost-instant snack.

pizza basics

making pizzas & flatbreads

While any kind of bread-making may have the reputation of being too time-consuming or difficult, once you have succeeded in producing a beautiful pizza or flatbread you will see what a misconception this is. Most pizza and flatbread recipes are easily divided into a series of small tasks, each one taking no more than a few minutes. Choose a recipe according to your needs. If you are in a hurry, you may wish to skip some steps by using store-bought pizza crust, pizza sauce, and pre-shredded mozzarella.

If you want to make your pizza dough ahead of time, it can be placed in the refrigerator to rise, as the cool temperature slows the rising process. Place the divided portions of dough in individual large sealable bags, pressing down the dough to flatten it into a disc and removing the air from the bags. Repeat this three times, at one-hour intervals. The dough can then be left in the refrigerator for up to 24 hours. When you want to use the dough, let it reach room temperature and rise for an additional 2 to 3 hours.

If you are making the dough the day you plan to make your pizzas, be sure to leave enough time for the dough to rise. This time can vary from 10 minutes to 2 to 3 hours depending on the dough you are making. Yeasted dough should be covered lightly and placed in a warm, draft-free place to rise. If you live in a cold climate and your kitchen is cool and drafty, turn on your oven to 350°F (175°C) as you begin preparing the dough. Let the oven heat up for 5 minutes, and then turn it off completely. Once you have prepared the dough, place it in the oven to rise, checking that the oven is just warm and not actually hot enough to bake your dough.

When rolling out dough, let it rest for a few minutes after you have rolled it once. Allow dough to relax into its new shape for 1 to 2 minutes, then continue rolling.

preparing to bake

Make sure to read through the recipe well before you plan to bake, to establish how long you will need to get from start to finish as well as to verify that you have all the necessary ingredients on hand. Baking involves using many kitchen surfaces for all the various steps, so it is always a good idea to start with a clean kitchen.

Once you have read through the recipe and have all the ingredients on hand, you are ready to start! The oven temperatures in recipes are listed before placing the pizza or flatbread in the oven, but to achieve the classic crispy-based crust, you need to have a very hot preheated oven and baking stone. Place the baking stone or tiles in the oven, to preheat for an hour. Use the hottest temperature on your oven, either 500°F (250°C) or 550°F (300°C). If you are uncertain about your oven's accuracy, use an oven thermometer, sold in hardware stores or kitchen stores. If you find your pizza crust is burning on the bottom before the top has cooked, reduce the oven temperature by 25-50°F (5-10°C) or raise the baking stone by one level.

Prepare your sauce and all the toppings while the dough is rising, and work quickly once your pizza crust has been placed on the peel. Gently shake your pizza peel to make sure the dough is not sticking and will transfer easily to the stone. Add a little flour or cornmeal to the peel to prevent sticking, or place a sheet of parchment paper on the peel under the crust. Pizzas and flatbreads bake quickly on a hot baking stone, so stay in the kitchen and keep an eye on how it is doing for your first few attempts. You may need to adjust the oven temperature or time depending on how your oven works.

basic pan pizza crust

This pizza dough makes one large rectangular pizza crust, or two 9-in. (23-cm.) round crusts.

1 cup bread flour
1 1/3 cups all-purpose flour
3/4 cups plus 1 tbsp. warm water
1 tsp. traditional active dry yeast

1/2 tsp. honey
1 1/2 tsp. olive oil
3/4 tsp. salt

To prepare the dough, combine the flour. Place warm water, yeast, honey, and olive oil in bowl of standing mixer. Add 1/3 cup flour and mix on low speed or whisk by hand until smooth. Cover with clean paper towel and let sit for 20 minutes, until mixture is foamy on top. Add remaining flour and salt and mix with dough hook for 4 minutes, or knead by hand for 10 minutes, until all the flour is incorporated and the dough is smooth. Cover with clean paper towel and place in a warm spot to rise for 1 1/2 hours, or until dough has almost doubled in size.

If making one pizza, lightly oil a rectangular baking pan (15 1/4 x 10 1/4 x 3/4 in. (38.7 x 26 x 1.91 cm.)). Place dough in pan, and punch down once in the center. Using your hands, stretch out the dough from the center to the sides, taking care to distribute it evenly around the pan. Using toothpicks or small lightweight containers as supports in each corner, tent the dough with paper towels and return to warm spot for another 45 minutes.

If making 2 pizzas, lightly oil two 9-in. (23-cm.) round cake pans. Using your hands or a rolling pin, stretch out each ball to form a 9-in. (23-cm.) disc. With fingers, work a little extra dough to edges to form crust. Place dough in pans, cover with clean paper towel, and return to warm spot for 45 minutes.

basic thin pizza crust

This crust rises only once and bakes in minutes, making it the quickest crust to make. It can be made into three 12-in. (30-cm.) pizzas, as described below, or divided into six individual 6-in. (15-cm.) pizzas. Baking time remains consistent.

1 1/2 cups all-purpose flour
1 1/2 cups bread flour
1 tsp. granulated sugar
1 tsp. quick-rise yeast

1 tsp. salt
1 1/2 tbsp. extra-virgin
    olive oil
1 cup very warm water

To prepare the pizza dough, combine 2 cups of the flour with the sugar, yeast, and salt in bowl of standing mixer. Set aside. Combine olive oil and warm water. With paddle attachment, slowly stir the water and oil into the flour mixture until well combined. Mix in 1 cup flour.

Change to dough hook attachment and knead on low for 4 to 5 minutes, until dough comes together as a ball and is smooth and elastic. If not using a standing mixer, turn dough onto a lightly floured surface and knead by hand for about 10 minutes.

Place dough in lightly oiled bowl and cover with clean paper towel. Set aside in a warm spot for 1 1/2 to 3 hours, until dough has almost doubled in volume.

Once dough has risen, use a sharp knife to divide the ball into 3 equal pieces. Shape each into a ball, and flatten to form a disc. Using fingers or rolling pin, stretch out each disc to 12-in. (30-cm.) rounds and very thin — about 1/12 in (0.5 cm.).

basic calzone crust

This dough is used for all the calzone recipes in this book.

1 1/2 cups all-purpose flour
1 1/2 cups bread flour
1 tsp. granulated sugar
2 tsp. quick-rise yeast

1 tsp. salt
1 1/2 tbsp. extra-virgin
   olive oil
1 cup warm water

To prepare the calzone dough, combine 2 cups of the flour with the sugar, yeast, and salt in bowl of standing mixer. Set aside. Combine olive oil and warm water. Using paddle attachment, slowly stir the water and oil into the flour mixture until well combined. Mix in 1 cup of flour.

Change to dough hook attachment and knead on low for 4 to 5 minutes, until dough comes together as a ball and is smooth and elastic. If not using a standing mixer, turn onto a lightly floured surface and knead by hand for about 10 minutes. Place dough in lightly oiled bowl and cover with clean paper towel. Set aside for 10 minutes.

When the dough has rested for 10 minutes, punch it down. Using a sharp knife, cut the dough into 4 equal pieces. Shape each into a ball, flatten down to form a disc, and lightly flour each disc.

On a lightly floured surface, roll out each disc 1/8 in. (0.5 cm.) thick and 6 in. (15 cm) round. Add flour as necessary to prevent sticking.

basic double pizza crust

This is the right crust for rustic and other stuffed pizzas.

2 tsp. active dry yeast
1 1/3 cups warm water
2 tbsp. olive oil

2 cups all-purpose flour
1 1/2 cups bread flour
1 tsp. salt

To make the dough, sprinkle yeast over warm water and set aside for a minute, or until yeast becomes foamy. Stir to completely dissolve yeast. Add olive oil to yeast mixture.

Combine flours and salt in large bowl of standing mixer. Add the yeast mixture and, using dough hook attachment, run machine on low speed for 4 to 5 minutes, or until dough forms a ball.

If making dough by hand, stir yeast mixture into flour until dough forms, then turn onto a lightly floured surface and knead for 10 minutes, until dough is smooth and elastic.

Place dough in lightly oiled bowl and cover with clean paper towel. Set aside in a warm spot for 1 1/2 to 2 hours, until dough has almost doubled in volume.

Punch down dough. Using a sharp knife, cut the dough in 2 pieces, one slightly larger than the other. Shape each piece into a ball. Place balls in lightly floured cake pans, tent the pans with a clean paper towel, and return to warm spot for an additional hour. Dough should almost double in size again.

basic neapolitan pizza crust

A delicious foolproof dough that makes enough for two 12-in. (30-cm.) pizzas.

1 tsp. dry active yeast	2 cups bread flour
1 1/4 cups warm water	1 cup all-purpose flour
1 tsp. salt	

To prepare the dough, sprinkle yeast over warm water in bowl of standing mixer and set aside for 5 minutes. Add salt, then mix in flour 1 cup at a time. When dough is beginning to form, change to dough hook attachment, and run mixer for 4 to 5 minutes, until dough is smooth and elastic.

Divide dough in 2 pieces and place in lightly oiled bowls. Roll dough around so each ball is lightly covered in oil.

Cover bowls with clean paper towels and place in warm spot to rise for 2 to 3 hours, until dough has almost doubled in size. If you prefer to make the dough the night before you plan to use it, seal bowls with plastic wrap and place in refrigerator. Remove from refrigerator one hour before you plan to use the dough.

Place pizza stone in oven and preheat oven to 500°F (250°C). Lightly dust each ball with flour. Using fingers or rolling pin, stretch out each ball to form a large circle, roughly 12 in. (30 cm.) in diameter.

basic turkish pizza crust

This dough is used for the Turkish pizza recipe in International Pizzas (page 114), but you can use it for individual pizzas as well. It contains more fat than other pizza doughs, resulting in a slightly softer, more pliable crust.

1 envelope (2 1/4 tsp.) active dry yeast
1 cup warm water
2 tbsp. unsalted butter, melted
2 tbsp. extra-virgin olive oil

1 tsp. salt
2 cups all-purpose flour
1 cup bread flour

To prepare the dough, sprinkle the yeast over the warm water in large bowl of standing mixer. Stir to mix and set aside for 10 minutes, until yeast has dissolved.

Mix in melted butter and olive oil. Add salt, then mix in flour 1 cup at a time. When dough begins to form, change to dough hook attachment, and run mixer for 4 to 5 minutes, until dough is smooth and elastic.

Place dough in lightly oiled bowl. Roll dough around so ball is lightly covered with oil.

Cover bowl with clean paper towel and place in warm spot to rise for 1 hour, until dough has almost doubled in size.

basic chicago deep-dish pizza crust

For all your deep-dish pizza cravings!

2 envelopes quick-rise yeast
   (2 1/4 tsp. each.)
2 cups warm water
1/2 cup canola oil

4 tbsp. olive oil
1/2 cup fine cornmeal
2 tsp. salt
5 1/2 cups all-purpose flour

To prepare the dough, dissolve yeast over warm water in large bowl of standing mixer. Let stand for 2 minutes. Add oil, cornmeal, salt, and 3 1/2 cups flour. Mix well.

Attach dough hook and mix in remaining flour. Knead for 4 to 5 minutes, until dough is smooth.

Cover bowl with paper towel and place in warm, draft-free spot to rise for 1 hour, until dough has doubled.

Punch down dough once, cover, and return to warm spot for additional 40 minutes. Divide dough into 3 equal pieces and shape each into a ball.

Makes three 9-in. (23-cm.) crusts

basic whole-wheat thin pizza crust

Whole-wheat flour offers more fiber and results in a crust with a slightly coarser texture.

1 cup all-purpose flour
1 cup bread flour
1 cup whole-wheat flour
1 tsp. granulated sugar

1 tsp. quick-rise yeast
1 tsp. salt
1 1/2 tbsp. extra-virgin olive oil
1 cup very warm water

To prepare the pizza dough, combine 2 cups of the flour with the sugar, yeast, and salt in bowl of standing mixer. Set aside. Combine olive oil and warm water. With paddle attachment, slowly stir the water and oil into the flour mixture until well combined. Mix in 1 cup flour.

Change to dough hook attachment and knead on low for 4 to 5 minutes, until dough comes together as a ball and is smooth and elastic. If not using a standing mixer, turn dough onto a lightly floured surface and knead by hand for about 10 minutes.

Place dough in lightly oiled bowl and cover with clean paper towel. Set aside in a warm spot for 1 1/2 to 3 hours, until dough has almost doubled in volume.

Once dough has risen, use a sharp knife to divide the ball into 3 equal pieces. Shape each into a ball, and flatten to form a disc. Using fingers or rolling pin, stretch out each disc to 12-in. (30-cm.) rounds and very thin — about 1/12 in. (0.5 cm.).

basic gluten-free pizza crust

This crust will make a satisfying pizza base replacement for those who observe a gluten-free diet.

2 tbsp. quick-rise yeast
1 tsp. sugar
1 1/3 cups warm milk
1 1/3 cups brown rice flour
1 cup tapioca flour

4 tsp. guar gum
1 tsp. salt
2 tsp. unflavored gelatin powder
2 tsp. extra-virgin olive oil
2 tsp. apple cider vinegar

Preheat oven to 425°F (220°C). In small bowl, sprinkle yeast and sugar over warm milk. Set aside for 5 minutes, until yeast and sugar have dissolved. In large bowl of standing mixer, combine flours, guar gum, salt, and gelatin powder. Add yeast mixture and mix until well incorporated. Mix in oil and vinegar.

Cover bowl with plastic wrap and let rise for 10 minutes. Line 12-in. (30-cm.) pizza pan with parchment paper. Turn dough into pizza pan and sprinkle with rice flour.

Using hands, press dough down to cover surface of pan.

Prebake 10 minutes before adding toppings.

Return to oven with toppings for 15 minutes. Add cheese and bake for 5 minutes longer.

basic pizza sauce

This simple and delicious sauce is used as the base for most pizzas.

3 tbsp. olive oil
1 garlic clove, minced
28-oz. can whole tomatoes
1/2 tsp. salt

1/2 tsp. dried oregano or 1 tbsp chopped
   fresh oregano
pinch of crushed red pepper flakes

To prepare the sauce, heat oil in large heavy frying pan.

Add garlic and cook for 1 to 2 minutes. Add tomatoes and break them up into small chunks with wooden spoon.

Simmer for 15 to 20 minutes, until most of the liquid has evaporated and sauce has thickened. Add salt, oregano, and red pepper flakes to taste.

Makes approximately 1 2/3 cups sauce

basic pesto

Fresh and fragrant, pesto is easy to make, and it's a delicious addition to pizzas and many flatbreads.

3 cups loosely packed fresh basil leaves
1/3 cup pine nuts
1/4 cup finely grated Parmesan

1/4 cup finely grated Romano
1/3 cup extra-virgin olive oil
salt and freshly ground black pepper

To make pesto, combine all ingredients except olive oil, salt and pepper in food processor or blender. Run machine until everything is finely chopped. With machine still operating, add olive oil in a thin stream until pesto becomes a smooth pastelike consistency. Season to taste with salt and pepper.

For a bright green pesto that does not discolor, blanche the basil leaves (submerge them in boiling water for a few seconds, until leaves brighten) before proceeding with the recipe.

Leftovers can be refrigerated for up to one week or frozen in ice cube trays for easy defrosting. Defrosted pesto may need to be returned to the food processor to restore its original texture.

Makes approximately 2 cups pesto

basic tapenade

This olive-based spread from Provence makes an appetizing alternative to regular pizza sauce. It can also make a tasty dip for pitas.

4 oz. anchovy fillets, rinsed and drained
4 peeled garlic cloves
3 cups pitted black olives

1 cup drained capers
1 cup extra-virgin olive oil
juice of 1 lemon

Combine all ingredients except lemon juice and olive oil in food processor. Process until smooth.

With machine running, pour olive oil in a continuous stream through chute.

Add lemon juice. Process until mixture is thick and smooth.

Leftovers may be stored in the fridge for up to one week.

basic sausage sauce

This sauce takes more time to make than the basic pizza sauce, but it is definitely worth the wait! Use hot or mild sausage, according to your tastes.

1 tbsp. olive oil
1 lb. Italian sausage
2 garlic cloves, minced
28-oz. can whole tomatoes
1/2 tsp. salt

1/2 tsp. dried oregano or 1 tbsp chopped fresh oregano
pinch of crushed red pepper flakes

To prepare the sauce, heat oil in large heavy frying pan. Remove sausage from casings and break into small chunks. Add sausage to pan and cook until lightly browned.

Stir in garlic and oregano and cook for 1 to 2 minutes. Add tomatoes and break them up into small chunks with wooden spoon.

Simmer for at least 1 hour, until most of the liquid has evaporated and sauce has thickened. Add salt and red pepper flakes to taste.

Makes approximately 1 2/3 cups sauce

basic ratatouille

This Provençal stew makes a delectable pizza topping, especially if you want more vegetables.

3 tbsp. extra-virgin olive oil
1 yellow onion, chopped
2 small eggplants, ends trimmed and chopped
2 garlic cloves, minced
3 small zucchini, ends trimmed and chopped
1 green bell pepper, seeded and chopped
1 red pepper, seeded and chopped

3 fresh thyme sprigs
1 fresh rosemary sprig
1 bay leaf
28-oz. can whole tomatoes
3 tbsp. roughly chopped fresh basil
salt and freshly ground black pepper

In large pot, heat oil over medium heat. Add onion and cook until softened and turning brown, 8 to 10 minutes. Add eggplant and garlic; continue cooking for 4 to 5 minutes. Stir in zucchini and peppers; sauté for 5 minutes.

Place thyme, rosemary, and bay leaf in a small cheesecloth bag, or simply tie together with kitchen twine to make a bouquet garni.

Add tomatoes and bouquet garni, and reduce heat to medium low. Cover saucepan and simmer for 30 to 40 minutes, stirring occasionally.

Remove bouquet garni and bay leaf. Stir in basil and season to taste.

pan pizzas

With a thick crust (soft inside and crispy outside) and layers of tomato sauce, melted cheese, and delicious toppings, these pan pizzas will please a crowd or satisfy a hungry family.

classic cheese pizza

see variations page 48

When you want a classic, this is where to start!

1 recipe basic pan pizza crust
   (page 16)
1 recipe basic pizza sauce
   (page 25)
1 1/2 cups shredded mozzarella

Follow the instructions on page 16 for making a rectangular pizza crust.

Preheat oven to 550°F (300°C). Spread sauce evenly over the pizza crust, leaving a 1/2-in. (1-cm.) border around the edge. Place on bottom rack in oven and bake for 8 minutes. Remove from oven and spread shredded mozzarella evenly over sauce.

Return to oven and bake for another 5 to 6 minutes, until cheese has melted and crust is golden brown.

Remove from oven and let stand for 5 minutes. Slice into 12 squares and serve immediately.

Makes 1 large rectangular pizza. Serves 6–8.

grilled chicken & fontina pizza

see variations page 49

This is an excellent way to add appeal to leftover grilled chicken.

1 recipe basic pan pizza crust (page 16)
1/2 recipe basic pizza sauce (page 25)
2 cups grated fontina cheese
2 cups grilled and sliced chicken breasts

2 thin slices red onion, rings separated
freshly ground black pepper
2 tbsp. finely chopped flat-leaf parsley
4 tbsp. finely grated Parmesan

Follow the instructons on page 16 for making 2 round pizza crusts.

Preheat oven to 550°F (300°C). Divide sauce between the 2 pans and spread thinly and evenly, leaving 1/2-in. (1-cm.) border around the edge.

Spread 1 cup grated fontina over the sauce on each pizza. Arrange half the onion rings and 1 cup chicken on each pizza. Lightly sprinkle each one with pepper.

Bake for 8 to 10 minutes on middle rack in oven, until cheese is melted and crust is golden brown. Sprinkle chopped parsley and Parmesan over pizzas.

Slice into wedges and serve.

Makes two 9-in. (23-cm.) pizzas. Serves 6–8.

pizza margherita

see variations page 50

Invented in 1889 and named for Queen Margherita, this pizza features the three colors of the Italian flag — red tomatoes, white mozzarella, and green basil.

1 recipe basic pan pizza crust (page 16)
1 recipe basic pizza sauce (page 25)
4 oz. baby bocconcini, sliced thin
    (or sliced mozzarella)
4 large basil leaves, roughly torn

Follow the instructions on page 16 for making 2 round pizza crusts.

Preheat oven to 550°F (300°C). Divide sauce between the 2 pans and spread evenly, leaving 1/2-in. (1-cm.) border around the edge.

Distribute cheese slices around the 2 pizzas.

Bake for 8 to 10 minutes on rack in lower half of oven, until cheese is melted and crust is golden brown. Sprinkle pieces of basil over pizzas.

Slice into wedges and serve.

Makes two 9-in. (23-cm.) pizzas. Serves 6–8.

sausage & pepper pizza

see variations page 51

Spicy sausage chunks and red pepper slices make this pizza burst with flavor.

1 recipe basic pan pizza crust (page 16)
1 lb. Italian sausage (mild or hot to suit
   your tastes)
1 tbsp. olive oil

1 recipe basic pizza sauce (page 25)
2 cups shredded mozzarella
1 red bell pepper, seeded and thinly
   sliced crosswise

Follow the instructions on page 16 for making a rectangular pizza crust.

Preheat oven to 550°F (300°C). Remove sausage from casings to form small chunks. Heat olive oil in large skillet and brown sausage. Remove sausage from pan and drain. Spread sauce evenly over the pizza crust, leaving a 1/2-in. (1-cm.) border around the edge.

Place on bottom rack in oven and bake for 8 minutes. Remove from oven and spread shredded mozzarella evenly over sauce. Arrange sausage chunks and red pepper slices on top.

Return to oven and bake for another 5 to 6 minutes, until cheese has melted and crust is golden brown.

Remove from oven and let stand for 5 minutes. Slice into 12 squares and serve immediately.

Makes 1 large rectangular pizza. Serves 6–8.

vegetarian pizza

see variations page 52

Overflowing with fresh tomatoes, mushrooms, onions, peppers, and green and black olives, this pizza is a vegetable lover's dream.

1 recipe basic pan pizza crust
   (page 16)
1 recipe basic pizza sauce
   (page 25)
2 cups shredded mozzarella

2-3 vine-ripened tomatoes,
   sliced
1 cup sliced mushrooms
1 yellow onion, thinly sliced

1 green bell pepper, thinly
   sliced
1/2 cup sliced Manzanilla
   olives
1/2 cup sliced black olives

Follow the instructions on page 16 for making a rectangular pizza crust.

Preheat oven to 550°F (300°C). Spread sauce evenly over the pizza crust, leaving a 1/2-in. (1-cm.) border around the edge. Place on bottom rack in oven and bake for 8 minutes.

Remove from the oven and spread shredded mozzarella evenly over sauce. Arrange the fresh tomato, mushroom, onion, pepper, and olive slices over cheese. Return to oven and bake for another 5 to 6 minutes, until the cheese has melted and crust is golden brown.

Remove from the oven and let stand for 5 minutes. Slice into 12 squares and serve immediately.

Makes 1 large rectangular pizza. Serves 6–8.

classic pan pizza with the works

see variations page 53

"Pizza with the works" traditionally refers to pizza with the combination of cheese, pepperoni, onion, mushrooms, and green peppers. Try some of our variations for tasty extras.

1 recipe basic pan pizza crust
  (page 16)
1 recipe basic pizza sauce
  (page 25)

2 cups shredded mozzarella
8 oz. pepperoni, thinly sliced
8 oz. white or button
  mushrooms, sliced

1/2 large yellow onion,
  thinly sliced
1 large green pepper, seeded
  and thinly sliced crosswise

Follow the instructions on page 16 for making a rectangular pizza crust.

Preheat oven to 550°F (300°C). Spread sauce evenly over the pizza crust, leaving a 1/2-in. (1-cm.) border around the edge. Place on bottom rack in oven and bake for 8 minutes.

Remove from oven and spread shredded mozzarella evenly over sauce. Arrange pepperoni, onion, mushroom, and pepper slices on top.

Return to oven and bake for another 5 to 6 minutes, until cheese has melted and crust is golden brown. Remove from oven and let stand for 5 minutes.

Slice into 12 squares and serve immediately.

Makes 1 large rectangular pizza. Serves 6–8.

garlic & olive oil pizza

see variations page 54

Slice this pizza in fingers and serve as an alternative to garlic bread.

1 recipe basic pan pizza crust (page 16)
2 garlic cloves, minced
2 tbsp. extra-virgin olive oil

1/2 tsp. dried oregano
pinch of crushed red pepper flakes
pinch of coarse salt

Follow the instructions on page 16 for making 2 round pizza crusts.

Combine the garlic, oil, and seasonings, and divide between the 2 pizzas.

Spread sauce around, leaving 1/2-in. (1-cm.) border.

Bake on bottom rack in oven for 7 to 9 minutes, until crust is golden brown. Let stand
5 minutes, slice into wedges or fingers, and serve.

Makes two 9-in. (23-cm.) pizzas. Serves 6–8.

steak & mushroom pizza

see variations page 55

This hearty pizza is guaranteed to satisfy the biggest appetites!

1 recipe basic pan pizza crust (page 16)
1 recipe basic pizza sauce (page 25)
12 oz. lightly grilled beef steak (flank or
    sirloin), thinly sliced

8 oz. white or brown mushrooms, thinly sliced
1 cup shredded mozzarella
1 cup grated smoked Gruyère
1/2 tsp. dried oregano (optional)

Follow the instructions on page 16 for making 2 round pizza crusts.

Preheat oven to 550°F (300°C). Divide sauce between the 2 pans and spread evenly, leaving 1/2-in. (1-cm.) border around the edge. Arrange steak and mushroom slices on both pizzas.

Combine grated cheeses and divide evenly between the 2 pans.

Bake for 8 to 10 minutes on rack in lower half of oven, until cheese is melted and crust is golden brown. Sprinkle with oregano if desired.

Slice into wedges and serve.

Makes two 9-in. (23-cm) pizzas. Serves 6–8.

caramelized onion, anchovy & olive pizza

see variations page 56

The sweetness of the caramelized onions offers the perfect complement to the salty anchovies and olives in this sophisticated pizza.

1 recipe basic pan pizza crust
   (page 16)
4-5 tbsp. extra-virgin olive oil
4 yellow onions, thinly sliced
4 tbsp. butter

1/4 tsp. dried rosemary,
   crumbled
salt and freshly ground black
   pepper

8-10 anchovies, drained
1/2 cup pitted kalamata olives
1/2 cup grated pecorino cheese
   grated

Follow the instructions on page 16 for making a rectangular pizza crust.

Preheat oven to 550°F (300°C). Warm oil in large heavy skillet. Add onions. Cook for 5 minutes or until onions soften. Add butter and rosemary and cook over low heat for 15 minutes, or until onions have caramelized. Add pinch of salt and pepper; let cool. Spread caramelized onions over pizza dough, leaving 1/2-in. (1-cm.) border around the edge. Arrange anchovies and olives on top. Place on bottom rack in oven and bake for 8 minutes. Remove from oven and sprinkle with grated pecorino cheese. Return to oven and bake for another 5 to 6 minutes, until cheese has melted and crust is golden brown. Remove from oven and let stand for 5 minutes. Slice into 12 squares and serve immediately.

Makes 1 large rectangular pizza. Serves 6–8.

seafood pizza

see variations page 57

This exquisite pizza needs only a mixed green salad to complete it.

1 recipe basic pan pizza crust (page16)
2 tbsp. extra-virgin olive oil
1 garlic clove, minced
2 cups cleaned squid rings
1 cup shelled and deveined shrimp

1 cup shucked clams
salt and freshly ground black pepper
2 tbsp. chopped flat-leaf parsley
2 tsp. grated lemon zest

Follow the instructions on page 16 for making a rectangular pizza crust.

Preheat oven to 550°F (300°C). Heat olive oil in large nonstick skillet. Add garlic and cook for 1 minute. Add seafood and cook for 1 to 2 minutes, until shrimp have turned pink and squid is opaque. Spread seafood around pizzas, leaving 1/2-in. (1-cm.) border.

Sprinkle with salt and freshly ground pepper. Bake on middle rack in oven for 8 to 10 minutes, until crust is golden brown.

Let stand 5 minutes. Sprinkle with parsley and lemon zest. Slice into wedges and serve immediately.

Makes two 9-in. (23-cm.) pizzas. Serves 6–8.

variations

classic cheese pizza

see base recipe page 31

pepperoni & cheese pizza
Prepare the basic recipe, adding 12 to 14 thin slices (or 4 oz.) of pepperoni over the sauce before adding the cheese.

salami & cheese pizza
Prepare the basic recipe, adding 3 to 4 slices salami, quartered into triangles, over the shredded cheese.

prosciutto & cheese pizza
Prepare the basic recipe, adding 3 to 4 slices prosciutto, torn into strips, over the sauce before adding the cheese.

pancetta & cheese pizza
Prepare the basic recipe, adding 2 oz. pancetta, cubed and fried until crispy, over the shredded cheese.

parma ham & cheese pizza
Prepare the basic recipe, adding 3 to 4 slices Parma ham, torn into strips, over the sauce before adding the cheese.

grilled chicken & fontina pizza

see base recipe page 32

bbq chicken & fontina pizza
Prepare the basic recipe, replacing the grilled chicken with an equal quantity of shredded rotisserie-barbecued chicken.

grilled chicken with sun-dried tomato pizza
Prepare the basic recipe, adding 4 drained and roughly chopped large sun-dried tomatoes (2 per pizza) over the layer of sauce. Omit red onion slices if desired.

grilled chicken & pesto pizza
Prepare the basic recipe, replacing the basic tomato sauce with 1/4 cup pesto (see page 26) per pizza. Omit fontina, red onion slices, and parsley. Garnish cooked pizza with 1/4 cup toasted pine nuts, if desired.

jerk chicken with monterey jack pizza
Prepare the basic recipe, replacing grilled chicken with an equal quantity of cooked and shredded jerk chicken. Replace fontina with an equal quantity of Monterey Jack cheese and substitute fresh cilantro for the parsley.

grilled chicken with crispy onion pizza
Prepare the basic recipe, replacing the red onion slices with 1/4 cup store-bought crispy onion topping (such as French's).

variations

pizza margherita

see base recipe page 35

pizza margherita on gluten-free pizza crust
Prepare the basic recipe, replacing the Basic Pan Pizza Crust with the Gluten-Free Pizza Crust (page 24).

pizza margherita with anchovies
Prepare the basic recipe, placing pieces of dried anchovies (approximately 6 pieces per pizza) over the sauce before adding the cheese.

pizza margherita with artichoke hearts
Prepare the basic recipe, adding 1/4 cup chopped and drained marinated artichoke hearts to each pizza, before adding the cheese.

pizza margherita with olives
Prepare the basic recipe, adding 1/4 cup chopped and drained marinated olives to each pizza, before adding the cheese.

pizza margherita with chèvre
Prepare the basic recipe, replacing the bocconcini with an equal quantity of sliced chèvre.

variations

sausage & pepper pizza

see base recipe page 36

sausage & sauerkraut pizza
Prepare the basic recipe, replacing the red pepper slices with 1/2 cup drained sauerkraut.

sausage pizza with mushroom ragout
Prepare the basic recipe, replacing the red pepper slices with 1/2 cup prepared creamed mushrooms.

sausage & pepper pizza with three onions
Prepare the basic recipe, replacing the red pepper slices with 1/4 small yellow onion, thinly sliced; 1/8 red onion, thinly sliced; and 1/8 Vidalia onion, thinly sliced.

sausage & chutney pizza
Prepare the basic recipe, replacing the basic pizza sauce with 1 1/2 cups chutney.

sausage & pepper pizza on gluten-free pizza crust
Prepare the basic recipe, replacing the Basic Pan Pizza Crust with the Gluten-Free Pizza Crust (page 24).

vegetarian pizza

see base recipe page 39

vegetarian pizza with asparagus
Prepare the basic recipe, adding 8 to 10 spears steamed asparagus with
the other toppings.

vegetarian pizza with feta
Prepare the basic recipe, replacing the mozzarella with 12 oz. crumbled feta.

vegetarian pizza with leeks
Prepare the basic recipe, adding 1 leek, which has been cut into matchsticks
and steamed until tender, with the other toppings.

vegetarian pizza with roasted root vegetables, pesto & chèvre
Prepare the basic recipe, replacing basic tomato sauce with 1/2 cup prepared
pesto. Replace mozzarella with 10 oz. crumbled soft unripened chèvre. Omit
the sliced tomatoes, mushrooms, onions, peppers, and olives. Replace with
3 cups assorted roasted root vegetables, such as carrots, parsnips, and beets.

vegetarian pizza with smoked gruyère
Prepare the basic recipe, replacing 1 cup mozzarella with 1 cup grated
smoked Gruyère. Combine the cheeses before spreading them over sauce.

classic pan pizza with the works

see base recipe page 40

pizza with the works & bacon
Prepare the basic recipe, adding 4 slices fried, drained, and crumbled bacon with the other toppings.

pizza with the works & three peppers
Prepare the basic recipe, using only 1/2 green pepper, and adding thin slices of 1/2 yellow and 1/2 red pepper with the other toppings.

pizza with the works & sausage
Prepare the basic recipe, but add to he other toppings 8 oz. Italian sausage, which has been removed from its casings in small chunks, browned in 1 tablespoon olive oil, and drained.

pizza with the works & roast beef
Prepare the basic recipe, omitting pepperoni and adding 8 oz. sliced deli or leftover roast beef with the other toppings.

pizza with the works & cheese crust
Prepare the basic recipe, lightly glazing the edge of the crust with olive oil and sprinkling it with an additional 1/4 cup shredded mozzarella when adding the rest of the cheese.

variations

garlic & olive oil pizza

see base recipe page 43

garlic & olive oil pizza with flat-leaf parsley
Prepare the basic recipe, sprinkling 1 tablespoon chopped fresh flat-leaf parsley over each pizza after they have been removed from the oven.

garlic & olive oil pizza with cheese
Prepare the basic recipe, adding 3/4 cup shredded mozzarella over each pizza after 5 minutes baking. Return to oven for additional 3 to 5 minutes, until cheese is melted and crust is golden brown.

garlic & olive oil pizza with kalamata olives
Prepare the basic recipe, adding 1/4 cup halved and pitted kalamata olives to each pizza, after spreading the sauce.

garlic & olive oil pizza with shrimp
Prepare the basic recipe, adding 1/2 cup deveined, peeled, and cooked shrimp to each pizza, after spreading the sauce.

garlic & olive oil pizza with sesame seed crust
Prepare the basic recipe, lightly glazing each crust with olive oil and a sprinkling of 1 tablespoon sesame seeds before adding sauce.

steak & mushroom pizza

see base recipe page 44

steak & mushroom pizza with raclette cheese
Prepare the basic recipe, replacing the smoked Gruyère cheese with
an equal quantity of grated raclette cheese.

steak & mushroom pizza with onions
Prepare the basic recipe, adding 1/2 thinly sliced red onion with the
steak and mushrooms.

steak & eggplant pizza
Prepare the basic recipe, replacing the mushrooms with 1 small Italian
eggplant, which has been sliced and grilled.

steak & zucchini pizza
Prepare the basic recipe, replacing the mushrooms with 1 small zucchini,
which has been sliced lengthwise and grilled.

steak & mushroom pizza with herb crust
Prepare the basic recipe, lightly glazing the edge of the crust with olive oil
and sprinkling with 1/2 teaspoon Italian seasoning before adding the sauce.

variations

caramelized onion, anchovy & olive pizza

see base recipe page 45

caramelized onion & boursin pizza
Prepare the basic recipe, but replace the pecorino wih 10 oz. Boursin
(a soft herb cheese), in small chunks, scattered over the caramelized
onions, anchovies, and olives.

caramelized onion & gorgonzola pizza
Prepare the basic recipe, but replace the pecorino with 10 oz. Gorgonzola,
in small chunks, scattered over the caramelized onions, anchovies, and olives.

caramelized onion & mushroom pizza
Prepare the basic recipe, adding 1 cup sliced mushrooms to the onions
to be caramelized.

caramelized onion with smoked mackerel pizza
Prepare the basic recipe, replacing the anchovies with 8 oz. smoked
mackerel, roughly broken into pieces. Omit olives.

anchovy, olive & tomato pizza
Prepare the basic recipe, omitting caramelized onions. Lightly glaze crust
with extra-virgin olive oil and add 1 to 2 thinly sliced fresh tomatoes
with the anchovies and olives.

variations

seafood pizza

see base recipe page 46

clam pizza with roasted garlic
Prepare the basic recipe, omitting shrimp and squid, and doubling the quantity of clams. To prepare roasted garlic, place 3 heads of garlic, drizzled with olive oil, on a baking pan in a preheated 375°F (190°C) oven for 50 to 60 minutes. Let cool, and slice in half crosswise, between stem and base of bulbs, so that each clove is halved. Squeeze roasted garlic into bowl, add olive oil from pan, and mash with fork until smooth. Spread 1/4 to 1/3 cup garlic purée over each crust before adding the clams. Sprinkle with dried and crumbled oregano and 2 tablespoons grated Romano.

seafood pizza with tomatoes
Prepare the basic recipe, arranging 1 sliced tomato before adding seafood.

crab & chèvre pizza
Prepare the basic recipe, replacing seafood mixture with 7 oz. crabmeat blended with 5 oz. soft, unripened chèvre. Top with 2 diced and seeded plum tomatoes, and chopped kalamata olives if desired.

calamari pizza
Prepare the basic recipe, omitting shrimp and clams. Double quantity of squid (calamari). Once calamari is arranged on crust, dot with 2 to 4 oz. soft, unripened chèvre; sprinkle with dried and crumbled oregano; and chopped kalamata olives (if desired).

thin crust pizzas

These pizzas make elegant appetizers, speedy snacks, or great meals — the crust bakes quickly so they are ready before you know it. Spread out an assortment of toppings and let friends and family choose their own for an informal pizza night — the crust is popular with adults and kids alike.

spinach & feta pizza

see variations page 76

Creamy spinach makes a great alternative to tomato sauce.

1 recipe basic thin pizza crust (page 17)
1 lb. baby spinach
1 1/2 tbsp. extra-virgin olive oil
1 garlic clove, minced
1/2 cup ricotta cheese

1/2 tsp. dried oregano
pinch of nutmeg
salt and freshly ground black pepper
1 1/2 cups crumbled feta

Preheat oven to 500°F (250°C). Place a pizza stone or unglazed clay tiles on the bottom of gas oven or lowest rack of electric oven. Following instructions on page 17, make three 12-in. (30-cm.) discs of pizza dough. To make spinach topping, remove stems from spinach. Heat oil in large, heavy skillet over medium heat. Add minced garlic and cook for 1 minute. Add spinach and toss until all the leaves have wilted, 2 to 3 minutes. Let cool, and place on paper towel to squeeze out excess moisture. In a medium bowl, combine spinach and ricotta until smooth. Season with oregano, nutmeg, and salt and pepper to taste. Lightly dust pizza peel with flour or cornmeal. Place one disc of pizza dough on peel and spread 1/3 of the spinach (roughly 2/3 cup) over the dough, leaving 1/2-in. (1-cm.) border around the edge. Sprinkle with 1/2 cup crumbled feta and gently shake pizza from the peel to the stone or tiles. Bake for 5 to 7 minutes, until cheese is melting and crust is puffy around edges and crispy on the bottom. Slide the peel back under the pizza to remove from oven. Repeat with remaining 2 pizzas.

Makes three 12-in. (30-cm.) pizzas. Serves 6.

garden vegetable pizza

see variations page 77

The perfect pizza to make when gardens and markets are filled with beautiful produce.

1 recipe basic thin pizza crust (page 17)
1 large eggplant, sliced crosswise
2 cups sliced zucchini
1–2 tbsp. extra-virgin olive oil

salt and freshly ground black pepper
1 recipe basic pizza sauce (page 25)
2 large fresh tomatoes, sliced

8 oz. Boursin (soft unripened herb cheese)
2 tbsp. finely chopped assorted fresh garden herbs (basil, oregano, rosemary)

Preheat oven to 500°F (250°C). Place pizza stone or unglazed clay tiles on bottom of gas oven or lowest rack of electric oven. Following instructions on page 17, make three 12-in. (30-cm.) discs of pizza dough. To prepare the vegetables, heat grill pan or barbecue grill to medium-high heat. Working in batches, place eggplant and zucchini slices in pan or on grill, brush lightly with olive oil, and cook each side 3 to 4 minutes, until veggies are tender and grill-marked. Season with salt and pepper and set aside. Lightly dust pizza peel with flour or cornmeal. Place one disc of pizza dough on peel and spread 1/3 of the pizza sauce over the dough, leaving 1/2-in. (1-cm.) border around the edge. Arrange several slices of eggplant, zucchini and tomato over sauce. Dot with small chunks of Boursin and sprinkle with 1 teaspoon fresh herbs. Gently shake pizza from the peel to the stone or tiles. Bake 5 to 7 minutes, until cheese is melting and crust is puffy around edges and crispy on the bottom. Slide the peel back under the pizza to remove from oven and sprinkle with 1 teaspoon chopped fresh herbs. Repeat with remaining 2 pizzas.

Makes three 12-in. (30-cm.) pizzas. Serves 6.

pesto pizza

see variations page 78

Such a simple pizza, yet totally divine.

1 recipe basic thin pizza crust (page 17)
3/4 cup basic pesto (page 26)
2 fresh tomatoes, sliced thinly
1 1/2 cups shredded mozzarella

Preheat oven to 500°F (250°C). Place pizza stone or unglazed clay tiles on bottom of gas oven or lowest rack of electric oven.

Following instructions on page 17, make three 12-in. (30-cm.) discs of pizza dough. Lightly dust pizza peel with flour or cornmeal.

Place one 12-in. (30-cm.) disc of pizza dough on peel and spread 1/4 cup pesto over the dough, leaving 1/2-in. (1-cm.) border around the edge.

Arrange 6 to 8 slices of tomato and sprinkle 1/2 cup shredded mozzarella on top. Gently shake pizza from the peel to the stone or tiles.

Bake 4 to 6 minutes, until cheese is melting and crust is puffy around edges and crispy on the bottom. Slide the peel back under the pizza to remove from oven. Repeat with remaining 2 pizzas.

Makes three 12-in. (30-cm.) pizzas. Serves 6.

wild mushrooms on
whole-wheat crust pizza

see variations page 79

The earthy flavor of mixed mushrooms pairs perfectly with the whole-wheat crust.

1 recipe basic thin whole-wheat crust pizza
    recipe (page 23),
1 recipe basic pizza sauce (page 25)
1 tbsp. extra-virgin olive oil
3 garlic cloves, minced

2 lbs. assorted wild mushrooms (shiitake, oyster,
    cremini and portobello), wiped clean,
    stemmed, and sliced
1 1/2 lbs. button mushrooms, wiped clean,
    stemmed, and sliced
1/2 tsp. dried rosemary, crumbled
1 1/2 cups shredded mozzarella

Preheat oven to 500°F (250°C). Place pizza stone or unglazed clay tiles on bottom of gas oven or lowest rack of electric oven. Following instructions on page 23, make three 12-in (30-cm) discs of pizza dough. Heat olive oil in large, heavy skillet. Add garlic and cook for 1 minute. Add mushrooms and continue cooking for 15 minutes, until liquid has evaporated and mushrooms are tender. Lightly dust pizza peel with flour or cornmeal. Place one disc of pizza dough on peel and spread 1/3 of the pizza sauce over the dough, leaving 1/2-in. (1-cm.) border around the edge. Spread 1/3 of the mushroom mixture over the sauce, sprinkle with rosemary, and arrange 1/3 of the shredded mozzarella on top. Gently shake pizza from the peel to the stone or tiles. Bake 4 to 6 minutes, until cheese is melting and crust is puffy around edges and crispy on the bottom. Slide the peel back under the pizza to remove from oven. Repeat with remaining 2 pizzas.

Makes three 12-in. (30-cm.) pizzas. Serves 6.

four seasons pizza

see variations page 80

A visually stunning pizza that truly evokes the flavors of each season.

1 recipe basic thin pizza crust (page 17)
spring topping
1 lb. fresh asparagus, ends trimmed
winter topping
1 cup ricotta
1/4 cup finely grated Parmesan
pinch of nutmeg
salt and freshly ground pepper

summer topping
1 cup pesto (page 26)
fall topping
1 cup red pepper hummus

Preheat oven to 500°F (250°C). Place pizza stone or unglazed clay tiles on bottom of gas oven or lowest rack of electric oven. Following instructions on page 17, make three 12-in. (30-cm) discs of pizza dough. To prepare spring topping, steam asparagus until crisp-tender, 4 to 5 minutes. To prepare winter topping, combine ricotta, Parmesan, nutmeg, salt, and pepper in bowl. Lightly dust pizza peel with flour or cornmeal. Place one disc of pizza dough on peel and spread 1/3 of the ricotta mixture over 1/4 of the pizza surface, leaving 1/2-in. (1-cm.) border around the edge. Place 1/3 of the asparagus stalks over the next quarter, trimming the ends as necessary so each stalk fits nicely. Spread 1/3 cup pesto over third quarter and 1/3 cup red pepper hummus over the final quarter. Gently shake pizza from the peel to the stone or tiles. Bake 4 to 6 minutes, until crust is puffy around edges and crispy on the bottom. Slide the peel back under the pizza to remove from oven. Repeat with remaining 2 pizzas.

Makes three 12-in. (30-cm.) pizzas. Serves 6.

pizza bianca

see variations page 81

This twist on the classic white pizza hides wilted spinach between two sumptuous layers of cheese.

1 recipe basic thin pizza crust (page 17)
2 cups ricotta
2 tbsp. finely chopped fresh basil

salt and freshly ground black pepper
pinch of nutmeg
1 cup wilted and chopped spinach

1 1/2 cups shredded mozzarella
1/2 cup finely grated Parmesan

Preheat oven to 500°F (250°C). Place pizza stone or unglazed clay tiles on bottom of gas oven or lowest rack of electric oven. Following instructions on page 17, make three 12-in. (30-cm.) discs of pizza dough.

To prepare topping, combine ricotta and basil in a medium bowl. Season with salt, pepper, and nutmeg. Lightly dust pizza peel with flour or cornmeal. Place one disc of pizza dough on peel and spread 2/3 cup ricotta mixture over the dough, leaving 1/2-in. (1-cm.) border around the edge. Arrange 1/3 of the spinach over ricotta and top with 1/2 cup shredded mozzarella and 1/3 of the Parmesan. Gently shake pizza from the peel to the stone or tiles.

Bake 4 to 6 minutes, until cheese is melting and crust is puffy around edges and crispy on the bottom. Slide the peel back under the pizza to remove from oven. Repeat with remaining 2 pizzas.

Makes three 12-in. (30-cm.) pizzas. Serves 6.

tapenade pizza

see variations page 82

Tapenade, a rich dip originating from Provence, is traditionally made with black olives, capers, and anchovies. Variations can be found in gourmet and specialty food shops.

1 recipe basic thin pizza crust (page 17)
1 1/2 cups basic tapenade (page 27)
6 oz. chèvre

Preheat oven to 500°F (250°C). Place pizza stone or unglazed clay tiles on bottom of gas oven or lowest rack of electric oven.

Following instructions on page 17, make three 12-in. (1-cm.) discs of pizza dough. Lightly dust pizza peel with flour or cornmeal. Place one disc of pizza dough on peel and spread 1/2 cup tapenade over the dough, leaving 1/2-in. (1-cm.) border around the edge.

Distribute chèvre, in 1/2 teaspoon-sized chunks, over the tapenade. Gently shake pizza from the peel to the stone or tiles.

Bake 4 to 5 minutes, until cheese is melting and crust is puffy around edges and crispy on the bottom. Slide the peel back under the pizza to remove from oven. Repeat with remaining 2 pizzas.

Makes three 12-in. (30-cm.) pizzas. Serves 6.

smoked salmon & caper pizza

see variations page 83

The crust for this pizza bakes before you add the toppings, making it easy to assemble for a breakfast buffet or to serve in wedges as hors d'oeuvres.

1 recipe basic thin pizza crust (page 17)
1 cup cream cheese
1/2 cup sour cream
1 tbsp. chopped fresh dill

1 tsp. lemon juice
12 oz. smoked Atlantic salmon
6 tbsp. drained capers

Preheat oven to 500°F (250°C). Place pizza stone or unglazed clay tiles on bottom of gas oven or lowest rack of electric oven.

Following instructions on page 17, make three 12-in. (1-cm.) discs of pizza dough. Lightly dust pizza peel with flour or cornmeal. Place one disc of pizza dough on peel and gently shake pizza from the peel to the stone or tiles.

Bake 4 to 5 minutes. Let stand until pizza is cool to touch.

To prepare cream cheese spread, combine cream cheese, sour cream, dill, and lemon juice until smooth. Spread 1/3 of the cream cheese mixture over each pizza. Top each pizza with 4 oz. smoked salmon and 2 tablespoons capers.

Repeat with remaining 2 pizzas.

Makes three 12-in. (30-cm.) pizzas. Serves 6.

fresh tomato pizza

see variations page 84

This pizza should only be made with vine-ripened tomatoes in season, and ideally, eaten al fresco!

1 recipe basic thin pizza crust
    (page 17)
4 vine-ripened tomatoes,
    roughly chopped
4–5 fresh basil leaves, torn

1 clove garlic, minced
2 tbsp. extra-virgin olive oil
salt and freshly ground black
    pepper
2 cups shredded mozzarella

2 vine-ripened tomatoes,
    thinly sliced
2 tbsp. finely chopped fresh
    basil

Preheat oven to 500°F (250°C). Place pizza stone or unglazed clay tiles on bottom of gas oven or lowest rack of electric oven.

Following instructions on page 17, make three 12-in. (1-cm.) discs of pizza dough.

To make fresh tomato sauce, use immersion or traditional blender to purée chopped tomatoes, basil, garlic, and olive oil. Season with salt and pepper. Lightly dust pizza peel with flour or cornmeal. Place one disc of pizza dough on peel and spread 2/3 cup sauce over the crust. Sprinkle 2/3 cup shredded mozzarella over sauce. Arrange fresh tomato slices over the cheese. Gently shake pizza from the peel to the stone or tiles.

Bake 4 to 5 minutes. Sprinkle 2 teaspoons chopped basil over pizza. Repeat with remaining 2 pizzas.

Makes three 12-in. (30-cm.) pizzas. Serves 6.

chèvre, arugula & pear pizza

see variations page 85

The unusual combination of flavors makes this a remarkably refreshing pizza.

1 recipe basic thin pizza crust (page 17)
12 oz. chèvre
1/4 cup crème fraiche
3 firm, ripe pears, such as Bosc or Anjou,
    peeled, cored, and sliced

2 tsp. lemon juice
1/2 lb. baby arugula, cleaned,
    dried, and stemmed

Preheat oven to 500°F (250°C). Place pizza stone or unglazed clay tiles on bottom
of gas oven or lowest rack of electric oven.

Following instructions on page 17, make three 12-in. (1-cm.) discs of pizza dough.
Lightly dust pizza peel with flour or cornmeal and place one disc of pizza dough on peel.

In a bowl, combine chèvre and crème fraiche until smooth. Toss pear slices in lemon juice
to prevent discoloration. Spread 1/3 of the chèvre mixture over crust, leaving a 1/2-in.
(1-cm.) border around the edge. Arrange slices from 1 pear over chèvre mixture. Place
1/2 cup baby arugula leaves over pear slices. Gently shake pizza from the peel to the
stone or tiles.

Bake 4 to 5 minutes. Repeat with remaining 2 pizzas.

Makes three 12-in. (30-cm.) pizzas.

variations

spinach & feta pizza

see base recipe page 59

spinach, feta & sun-dried tomato pizza
Prepare the basic recipe, adding 2 large sun-dried tomatoes, drained
and chopped, to each pizza with the feta.

spinach, bacon & chèvre pizza
Prepare the basic recipe. Fry 12 slices bacon, then drain, crumble, and divide
into 3 portions. Add 1 portion to each pizza. Replace crumbled feta with an
equal quantity of chèvre.

spinach, feta & olive pizza
Prepare the basic recipe, adding 1/2 cup drained and chopped black olives
to each pizza with the feta.

creamy spinach & egg pizza
Prepare the basic recipe, reducing oven to 400°F (200°C). Cream the spinach
mixture in a food mill or with an immersion blender. Spread spinach over
crust and place in oven for 10 minutes. Remove from oven. Break an egg
over the middle of each pizza and return to oven for 5 minutes.

spinach, escarole & swiss chard pizza
Prepare the basic recipe, using 1/2 lb. of an assorted fresh greens: (spinach,
escarole, and Swiss chard) in place of the pound of spinach.

garden vegetable pizza

see base recipe page 60

garden vegetable pizza with cauliflower

Prepare the basic recipe. Roast 1/2 head of cauliflower, broken into florets, in 400°F (200°C) oven for 25 to 30 minutes. Add roasted cauliflower with other vegetables.

garden vegetable pizza with pesto

Prepare the basic recipe, replacing basic pizza sauce with 1/4 cup pesto (page 26) per pizza.

garden vegetable pizza with herb crust

Prepare the basic recipe, lightly glazing the edge of the pizza crusts with olive oil. Sprinkle each with 1/2 teaspoon Italian seasoning.

balsamic garden vegetable pizza

Prepare the basic recipe, tossing the vegetable slices in 2 tablespoons balsamic vinegar mixed with 4 tablespoons olive oil before grilling them.

spring vegetable pizza

Prepare the basic recipe, omitting the eggplant and zucchini. Steam 8 to 12 thin asparagus spears per pizza until crisp-tender. Arrange on each pizza along with 1/2 cup sliced mushrooms and 2 to 4 marinated artichoke hearts, drained and roughly chopped.

variations

pesto pizza

see base recipe page 63

pesto & artichoke heart pizza
Prepare the basic recipe, adding 3 to 4 drained and roughly chopped
marinated artichoke hearts to each pizza before adding the cheese.
Replace mozzarella with 4 to 5 teaspoon-sized chunks of chèvre if desired.

pesto & sun-dried tomato pizza
Prepare the basic recipe, replacing fresh tomato slices with 3 to 4 drained
and roughly chopped sun-dried tomatoes on each pizza.

pesto & roasted red pepper pizza
Prepare the basic recipe, adding 3 to 4 sections of roasted red pepper,
drained and cut into strips, to each pizza before adding the cheese.

pesto & roasted eggplant pizza
Prepare the basic recipe, adding 3 to 4 slices roasted eggplant, diced,
to each pizza before adding the cheese.

pesto pizza with sesame crust
Prepare the basic recipe, lightly glazing the edge of the crust with olive
oil and sprinkling with 1/2 teaspoon sesame seeds before adding the
pesto and toppings.

wild mushrooms on whole-wheat crust pizza

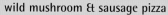

see base recipe page 64

wild mushroom & sausage pizza
Prepare the basic recipe. Remove 1 lb. Italian sausage from its casings in small chunks and brown in 1 to 2 tablespoons olive oil for, drained and divided between the 3 pizzas.

wild mushroom & sage pizza
Prepare the basic recipe, replacing the dried rosemary with 1/4 teaspoon dried or 1 teaspoon chopped fresh sage.

wild mushroom & tapenade pizza
Prepare the basic recipe, adding 8 half-teaspoon dollops of tapenade (page 27) per pizza over the shredded mozzarella.

wild mushroom & crème fraiche pizza
Prepare the basic recipe, omitting the mozzarella and adding 6 to 8 teaspoons of crème fraiche over the mushroom mixture.

wild mushrooms with chèvre and parsley on basic crust
Prepare the basic recipe, replacing the whole-wheat crust with the basic thin crust recipe. Omit the mozzarella and add 3 to 4 teaspoons of chèvre to each pizza over the mushroom mixture. Once pizzas have baked, sprinkle each with 1/4 teaspoon chopped fresh flat-leaf parsley.

variations

four seasons pizza

see base recipe page 66

spring pizza
Prepare the basic recipe, keeping only spring topping. Double quantity of asparagus and chop into 1-in. (2-cm.) pieces. Add 2 lbs. fresh leeks. Using only the white and pale green ends, clean and slice into matchstick-shaped pieces. Steam vegetables together, then toss in 3 tablespoons French vinaigrette. Spread 1/3 vegetable mixture over each pizza base.

summer pizza
Prepare the basic recipe, keeping only summer topping. Use 1 1/2 cups pesto and spread 1/2 cup over each pizza base. Garnish with fresh tomato slices if desired.

fall pizza
Prepare the basic recipe, keeping only fall topping. Use 1 1/2 cups red pepper hummus and spread 1/2 cup over each base. Add 1/2 sliced red pepper to each pizza before baking.

winter pizza
Prepare the basic recipe, keeping only winter topping. Use 3 cups ricotta and 3/4 cup grated Parmesan, and season with nutmeg, salt and pepper to taste. Spread 1/3 of the ricotta mixture over each pizza. Add 3 to 4 drained and chopped artichoke hearts per pizza, if desired.

variations

pizza bianca

see base recipe page 67

four-cheese pizza bianca
Prepare the basic recipe, replacing the cheese quantities with 3/4 cup
shredded mozzarella, 3/4 cup grated fontina, 1/4 cup grated Parmesan,
and 1/4 cup grated Romano.

pizza bianca with black olives
Prepare the basic recipe, adding 1/2 cup black olive slices per pizza over
the spinach mixture.

pizza bianca with shrimp
Prepare the basic recipe, adding 4 oz. peeled and cooked shrimp per pizza
over the spinach mixture.

pizza bianca with rosemary
Prepare the basic recipe, replacing basil with 1 teaspoon dried
rosemary, crumbled.

pizza bianca with sesame crust
Prepare the basic recipe, lightly glazing the 1/2-in. (1-cm.) border with extra-
virgin olive oil and sprinkling with 1/2 teaspoon sesame seeds per pizza.

variations

tapenade pizza

see base recipe page 69

tapenade pizza with roasted veggies
Prepare the basic recipe, adding 1/2 cup assorted roasted vegetables, such as red pepper, red onion, zucchini, and eggplant, per pizza, before adding the chèvre.

tapenade pizza with anchovies & red pepper
Prepare the basic recipe, adding 6 to 8 marinated anchovies, drained and patted dry, and 1/2 sliced red bell pepper per pizza before adding the chèvre.

tapenade pizza with bocconcini
Prepare the basic recipe, replacing the chèvre with an equal quantity of bocconcini.

tapenade pizza with feta & cherry tomatoes
Prepare the basic recipe, adding 6 to 8 cherry tomatoes per pizza. Slice tomatoes in half lengthwise and arrange them over the tapenade. Replace chèvre with an equal quantity of feta.

tapenade pizza with shiitake mushrooms
Prepare the basic recipe, adding 4 oz. shiitake mushroom caps per pizza. Slice mushroom in 1/2-in. (1-cm.) strips and arrange them over the tapenade.

variations

smoked salmon & caper pizza

see base recipe page 70

smoked mackerel pizza
Prepare the basic recipe, replacing the smoked salmon with an equal quantity of smoked mackerel.

smoked trout pizza
Prepare the basic recipe, replacing the smoked salmon with an equal quantity of smoked trout.

smoked salmon & red onion pizza
Prepare the basic recipe, adding 1/2 thinly sliced red onion, divided between the 3 pizzas.

smoked salmon & caper pizza on whole-wheat crust
Prepare the basic recipe, replacing the basic thin pizza crust with the whole-wheat thin pizza crust (page 23).

smoked salmon & fresh tomato pizza
Prepare the basic recipe, adding 1 thinly sliced fresh tomato, divided between the 3 pizzas.

variations

fresh tomato pizza

see base recipe page 73

fresh tomato pizza with saint-augur
Prepare the basic recipe, adding 4 oz. crumbled Saint-Agur cheese
over the sauce on each pizza. Omit mozzarella. Sprinkle each pizza
with 1/4 cup grated Parmesan before adding the chopped basil.

fresh tomato pizza with bocconcini
Prepare the basic recipe, replacing shredded mozzarella with 4 oz. sliced
bocconcini per pizza.

fresh tomato pizza with marinated artichoke hearts
Prepare the basic recipe, adding 3 to 4 marinated artichoke hearts, drained
and roughly chopped, per pizza. Place artichoke pieces over mozzarella
before baking.

fresh tomato pizza with pepperoni
Prepare the basic recipe, adding 6 to 8 slices of pepperoni per pizza.
Place pepperoni slices over mozzarella before baking.

fresh tomato pizza with oregano
Prepare the basic recipe, replacing the fresh basil leaves with 2 tablespoons
freshly chopped oregano and the chopped basil with 2 tablespoons freshly
chopped oregano.

chèvre, arugula & pear pizza

see base recipe page 74

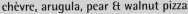

chèvre, arugula, pear & walnut pizza
Prepare the basic recipe, adding 2 tablespoons chopped walnuts to each pizza, over the arugula leaves.

chèvre, arugula & olive pizza
Prepare the basic recipe, omitting the pear slices. Add 2 tablespoons sliced black olives to each pizza before adding the arugula leaves.

chèvre, arugula & cremini mushroom pizza
Prepare the basic recipe, omitting the pear slices. Add 2 sliced cremini mushrooms per pizza, over the chèvre mixture.

chèvre, arugula, pear & prosciutto pizza
Prepare the basic recipe, adding 2 to 4 slices prosciutto, torn into strips, per pizza over the pear slices.

chèvre, arugula & pear pizza with balsamic vinegar
Prepare the basic recipe, drizzling each pizza with 2 teaspoons balsamic vinegar after they have been baked.

rustic pizzas & calzones

These hearty pizzas and calzones are pure comfort food. Overflowing with luscious cheeses and cured meats, they are the pizzas traditionally made by home cooks throughout Italy.

artichoke heart & ricotta calzones

see variations page 104

Be sure to seal your calzones tightly, so that none of the delicious filling leaks out during baking!

1 recipe basic calzone crust (page 18)
1 cup ricotta cheese
3/4 cup 1/4-in. (0.5-cm.) cubes mozzarella cheese
2 tbsp. finely grated Parmesan cheese

1/2 cup drained and roughly chopped marinated artichoke hearts
2 tbsp. flat-leaf finely chopped parsley
freshly ground black pepper

Preheat the oven to 450°F (230°C). While the dough is resting, prepare the filling. In a large bowl, combine the cheeses, artichoke hearts, and parsley. Add freshly ground black pepper to taste. Follow the instructions on page 18 for rolling out the dough into 4 equal discs. Using a pastry brush, glaze the top edge of the circles with water. Spoon 1/4 of the filling onto the lower half of each circle. Fold the top over so that the edge of the top sits 1/2 in. (1 cm.) away from the bottom half. Lightly glaze the edge of the top piece and fold the bottom over to seal tightly. Make a 1/2-in. (1-cm.) slit in the top to allow steam to escape. Place the calzones on a preheated baking stone or a cookie sheet lined with parchment paper and bake on the middle rack for 15 to 20 minutes, or until the filling is hot and the crust is golden brown.

Makes 4 calzones

rustic pancetta & mortadella pizza

see variations page 105

This pizza features a spectacular blend of smoked cheeses and cured meats.

1 recipe basic double pizza crust (page 19)
1–2 mild Italian sausages, removed from casings
1/4 lb. pancetta, cubed
1 tbsp. extra-virgin olive oil
1/4 lb. mortadella, cut into small pieces

1 cup ricotta cheese
1/4 cup smoked provolone cubes
1/2 cup shredded mozzarella
1/4 cup finely grated Parmesan
2 eggs, lightly beaten
1 garlic clove, minced

2 tbsp. chopped flat-leaf parsley
pinch crushed red pepper flakes
freshly ground black pepper

Preheat the oven to 400°F (200°C). While dough is in its second rising, make the filling. Fry the crumbled sausage meat and pancetta cubes in olive oil for 5 to 6 minutes, until sausage is cooked through (remove pancetta from pan earlier as it gets crispy). Drain and place in large bowl. Add mortadella, cheeses, eggs, garlic, and seasonings, and stir until well combined. On a lightly floured surface, roll out first ball of dough to a 12-in. (30-cm.) round. Add flour as necessary to prevent sticking. Place dough in a 9-in. (23-cm.) springform pan, so there is 1 in. (2 cm.) hanging over the edge. Pour filling into pan. Roll out second ball to a 9-in. (23-cm.) round and place over the filling. Fold the overhanging dough from the bottom crust over the edge of the top crust, pinching lightly to seal. Make 1 to 2 slits in the top to allow steam to escape. Bake in middle of oven for 45 minutes. Let sit 10 to 15 minutes before slicing into 8 wedges.

Makes one 9-in. (23-cm.) double-crusted pizza. Serves 8.

rustic ricotta & salami pizza

see variations page 106

This is similar to the Pancetta & Mortadella Pizza, but with the peppery accent of salami.

1 recipe basic double pizza crust (page 19)
1 cup ricotta cheese
1/2 lb. dry salami, sliced and cut into quarters
1 fresh tomato, chopped
1/4 cup smoked provolone cubes

1/2 cup shredded mozzarella
1/4 cup finely grated Parmesan
2 tbsp. chopped flat-leaf parsley
1 egg, lightly beaten

Preheat the oven to 400°F (200°C). While the dough is in its second rising, make the filling.

Combine all ingredients in a bowl. Stir to blend evenly. On a lightly floured surface, roll out first ball to a 12-in. (30-cm.) round. Add flour as necessary to prevent sticking. Place dough in a 9-in. (23-cm.) springform pan, so there is 1 in. (2 cm.) hanging over the edge. Pour filling into pan.

Roll out second ball to a 9-in. (23-cm.) round and place over the filling. Fold the overhanging dough from the bottom crust over the edge of the top crust, pinching lightly to seal. Make 1 to 2 slits in the top to allow steam to escape.

Bake in middle of oven for 45 minutes. Let sit 10 to 15 minutes before slicing into 8 wedges.

Makes one 9-in (23-cm.) double-crusted pizza. Serves 8.

shrimp panzerotti

see variations page 107

Shrimp in a creamy sauce make this savory turnover an indulgent treat.

1 recipe basic calzone crust
  (page 18)
1 1/2 lb. shrimp, cleaned,
  peeled, and deveined
1 cup dry white wine

1/4 cup chopped flat-leaf
  parsley
1/2 tsp. salt
2 tbsp. unsalted butter
2 cups sliced button
  mushrooms

2 green onions, chopped
3 tbsp. unsalted butter
3 tbsp. all-purpose flour
1/2 cup half-and-half cream
1/4 cup grated Fontina cheese

Preheat oven to 450°F (230°C). While the dough is resting, prepare the filling. In large
saucepan, combine shrimp, wine, and parsley. Add enough water to just cover the shrimp.
Bring to a boil and simmer for 5 to 6 minutes, until shrimp are pink and opaque. Remove
shrimp from liquid. Return liquid to boil. Cook until liquid has reduced to 1 cup. Strain
and set aside. Melt 2 tablespoons butter in saucepan. Sauté mushrooms and green onions
for 5 to 6 minutes, until mushrooms are tender. Set aside. Melt 3 tablespoons butter in
saucepan. Add flour, and stir until smooth paste begins to bubble. Using whisk, add reserved
wine liquid. Cook and stir for 1 minute. Add cream, shrimp, mushrooms, and cheese. Stir
until cheese has melted and mixture is heated evenly. Follow the instructions on page 18
for rolling out the dough into 4 equal discs. Using a pastry brush, glaze the top edge of the
circles with water. Spoon some filling onto the lower half of each circle — do not overstuff, as
they will leak. If there is extra filling, it can be served with the cooked panzerotti as a sauce.

Fold the top over so that the edge of the top sits 1/2 in. (1 cm.) away from the bottom half. Lightly glaze the edge of the top piece and fold the bottom over to seal tightly. Make a 1/2-in. (1-cm.) slit in the top to allow steam to escape. Place the calzones on a preheated baking stone or on a cookie sheet lined with parchment paper and bake on the middle rack for 15 to 20 minutes, or until the filling is hot and the crust is golden brown.

Makes 4 calzones

broccoli, asiago &
pine nut calzones

see variations page 108

These delectable calzones offer a nutritious boost from the broccoli and pine nuts.

1 recipe basic calzone crust (page 18)
2 florets from broccoli stalks, steamed until
   tender (or one 10 oz. package frozen
   broccoli florets, thawed and drained)
1 cup ricotta

1/2 cup shredded mozzarella
1/4 cup finely grated Asiago
1/2 cup pine nuts, toasted and roughly chopped
salt and freshly ground black pepper
pinch of gound nutmeg

Preheat oven to 450°F (230°C). While the dough is resting, prepare the filling. Chop broccoli florets and combine with cheeses and pine nuts. Season with salt, pepper, and nutmeg.

Follow the instructions on page 18 for rolling out the dough into 4 equal circles. Using a pastry brush, glaze the top edge of the circles with water. Spoon 1/4 cup filling onto the lower half of each circle. Fold the top over so that the edge of the top sits 1/2 in. (1 cm.) away from the bottom half. Lightly glaze the edge of the top piece and fold the bottom over to seal tightly. Make a 1/2-in. (1-cm.) slit in the top to allow steam to escape.

Place the calzones on a preheated baking stone or on a cookie sheet lined with parchment paper and bake on the middle rack for 15 to 20 minutes, or until the filling is hot and the crust is golden brown.

Makes 4 calzones.

mozzarella & ham stromboli

see variations page 109

A stromboli — a rolled pizza — is named for the volcanic island of Stromboli because of the way the cheese leaks out of the crust during baking.

1 recipe basic calzone crust (page 18)
4 cups shredded mozzarella
1/2 lb. deli ham, thinly sliced

2 tbsp. unsalted butter, melted
2 tbsp. finely grated Parmesan

Preheat oven to 375°F (190°C).

Punch down the dough. Using a sharp knife, divide it into 2 equal pieces. Shape each into a ball and roll out into two 14-in. (35-cm.) x 12-in. (30-cm.) rectangles.

Spread 2 cups shredded mozzarella over first rectangle, leaving a 1/2-in. (1-cm.) border. Top with half the ham slices. Starting from the long edge, roll tightly to form a long cylinder. Pinch seam to seal and fold ends under. Repeat process with the second ball of dough.

Brush each stromboli with 1 tablespoon melted butter and sprinkle each with 1 tablespoon grated Parmesan. Place the stromboli on a cookie sheet lined with parchment paper and bake on the middle rack for 20 to 25 minutes, or until the crust is golden brown.

Transfer to wire rack to cool for 5 minutes. Slice on the diagonal.

Makes 2 stromboli. Serves 6–8.

fontina & basil piadina

see variations page 110

Piadina are flatbreads that are baked quickly in a skillet and then folded over a simple filling. If you cannot find the authentic, semi-firm Fontina Valle d'Aosta, you can substitute the firm fontina found in most supermarkets, grated instead of crumbled.

3 1/2 cups all-purpose flour
1 tsp. salt
1/2 tsp. baking powder
1 cup warm water

1/4 cup extra-virgin olive oil
2 cups crumbled Fontina Valle d'Aosta
16 fresh basil leaves, torn into pieces

To prepare the dough, combine flour, salt, and baking powder in the bowl of a standing mixer. Add water and oil. Using dough hook, run mixer on low speed for 1 to 2 minutes, or until dough is smooth and elastic. Turn dough onto lightly floured surface and knead by hand for another 1 to 2 minutes. Shape dough into ball and place in lightly oiled bowl. Cover with paper towel and set aside for 30 to 60 minutes. Using a sharp knife, cut dough into 8 equal pieces. Shape each piece into a ball; keep the remaining pieces covered. Using a rolling pin, roll out each ball to 8 in. (20 cm.) round. Stack between sheets of parchment paper.

Heat nonstick skillet over medium-high heat. Place first piece of dough in skillet and cook for 30 seconds, until dough looks dry around the edges and is golden brown. Turn the piadina over and cook until second side is also golden brown. Remove piadina from pan, then fill with 1/4 cup Fontina and 2 torn fresh basil leaves. Repeat with remaining 7 rounds of dough.

Makes 8 piadina. Serves 8 as a light lunch or snack.

crab & italian parsley calzones

see variations page 111

The rich cream cheese and crab filling makes these calzones suitable for entertaining, but there is no reason not to enjoy them on a regular weeknight as well!

1 recipe basic calzone crust (page 18)
1 cup shredded mozzarella
1 cup cream cheese, softened
8 oz. crabmeat

4 green onions, finely chopped
1 clove garlic, minced
2 tbsp. finely chopped flat-leaf parsley

Preheat oven to 450°F (230°C). Follow the instructions on page 18 for rolling the dough into 4 equal circles.

Combine the cheeses, crabmeat, green onion, garlic, and parsley until well blended. Using a pastry brush, glaze the top edge of the dough circles with water. Spoon 1/4 cup filling onto the lower half of each circle.

Fold the top over so that the edge of the top sits 1/2 in. (1 cm.) away from the bottom half. Lightly glaze the edge of the top piece and fold the bottom over to seal tightly. Make a 1/2-in. (1-cm.) slit in the top to allow steam to escape.

Place the calzones on a preheated baking stone or on a cookie sheet lined with parchment paper and bake on the middle rack for 15 to 20 minutes, or until the filling is hot and the crust is golden brown.

Makes 4 calzones.

cheddar & bacon stuffed pizza

see variations page 112

The stuffed pizza is a close relative of the Chicago deep-dish pizza, and this double-crust pizza has a distinctly American flavor!

1 recipe basic double pizza crust (page 19)
1 cup ricotta cheese
1/2 lb. bacon, fried until crispy and crumbled
1/2 cup cheddar, cut into small cubes

1/4 cup shredded mozzarella
1/4 cup shredded Monterey Jack
1 egg, lightly beaten

Preheat the oven to 400°F (200°C). While dough is in its second rising, make the filling.

Combine all ingredients in a bowl. Stir to blend evenly. On a lightly floured surface, roll out first dough ball to a 12-in. (30-cm.) round. Add flour as necessary to prevent sticking.

Place dough in a 9-in. (23-cm.) springform pan, so there is 1 in. (2 cm.) hanging over the edge. Pour filling into pan.

Roll out second dough ball to a 9-in. (23-cm.) round and place over the filling. Fold the overhanging dough from the bottom crust over the edge of the top crust, pinching lightly to seal. Make 1 to 2 slits in the top to allow steam to escape.

Bake in middle of oven for 45 minutes. Let sit 10 to 15 minutes before slicing into 8 wedges.

Makes one 9-in. (23-cm.) stuffed pizza. Serves 8.

sausage & mushroom calzones

see variations page 113

With its combination of spicy and earthy flavors, this calzone is pure comfort food on a winter's evening.

1 recipe basic calzone crust
   (page 18)
12 oz. Italian sausage,
   removed from casings and
   crumbled

1 cup sliced mushrooms
1 tbsp. extra-virgin olive oil
1/2 recipe basic pizza sauce
   (page 25)
1 cup shredded mozzarella

2 tbsp. unsalted butter,
   melted
4 tsp. finely grated Parmesan

Preheat oven to 450°F (230°C). While the dough is resting, prepare the filling. Brown the crumbled sausage meat and mushroom slices in olive oil for 5 to 6 minutes, until sausage is cooked through. Add pizza sauce.

Follow the instructions on page 18 for rolling the dough into 4 equal circles. Using a pastry brush, glaze the top edge of the circles with water. Spoon 1/4 of the filling onto the lower half of each circle. Sprinkle with 1/4 cup mozzarella. Fold the top over so that the edge of the top sits 1/2 in. (1 cm.) away from the bottom half. Lightly glaze the edge of the top piece and fold the bottom over to seal tightly. Make a 1/2-in. (1-cm.) slit in the top to allow steam to escape. Brush tops with melted butter and sprinkle with 1 teaspoon Parmesan. Place the calzones on a preheated baking stone or on a cookie sheet lined with parchment paper and bake on the middle rack for 15 to 20 minutes, or until the filling is hot and the crust is golden brown.

Makes 4 calzones.

variations

artichoke heart & ricotta calzone

see base recipe page 87

artichoke heart calzones with four cheeses
Prepare the basic recipe, reducing amount of cubed mozzarella
to 1/4 cup and adding 1/4 cup cubed fontina in its place.

artichoke heart & ricotta calzones with pancetta
Prepare the basic recipe, adding 3 1/2 oz. cubed and fried pancetta
to the filling mixture.

artichoke heart calzones with garlic and pepper
Prepare the basic recipe, adding 1 minced clove garlic and a pinch
of crushed red pepper flakes to the filling mixture.

artichoke heart calzones with basil
Prepare the basic recipe, replacing the flat-leaf parsley with an equal
quantity of fresh basil.

artichoke heart calzones with white clams
Prepare the basic recipe, adding 1/2 cup of shucked, cleaned, and cooked
white clams to the filling mixture.

variations

rustic pancetta & mortadella pizza

see base recipe page 88

rustic parma ham & mortadella pizza
Prepare the basic recipe, replacing the pancetta with an equal quantity
of Parma ham, cut into small pieces.

rustic prosciutto & mortadella pizza
Prepare the basic recipe, replacing the pancetta with an equal
quantity of prosciutto, cut into small pieces.

rustic italian sausage pizza
Prepare the basic recipe, replacing the pancetta with 1 to 2 more
Italian sausages.

rustic pancetta & mortadella pizza with garlic & peppers
Prepare the basic recipe, sautéing 1/2 diced red bell pepper with the sausage
and pancetta. Add 1 additional minced clove of garlic to the filling.

rustic pancetta & five-cheese pizza
Prepare the basic recipe, adding 1/4 cup grated Romano to the filling.

rustic ricotta & salami pizza

see base recipe page 91

rustic ricotta & ground beef pizza
Prepare the basic recipe, replacing the salami with 1/2 lb. browned
and drained lean ground beef.

rustic ricotta & merguez pizza
Prepare the basic recipe, replacing the salami with 1/2 lb. Merguez sausage,
which has been removed from its casings, crumbled, browned, and drained.

rustic ricotta & roast vegetable pizza
Prepare the basic recipe, replacing the salami with 1 1/2 cups assorted
roasted vegetable chunks.

rustic ricotta & spinach pizza
Prepare the basic recipe, replacing the salami with 1 lb. steamed baby
spinach leaves. Add 1 minced clove garlic to the filling.

rustic ricotta & quinoa pizza
Prepare the basic recipe, replacing the salami with 1 cup cooked quinoa.
Replace flat-leaf parsley with equal quantity of cilantro, and add 1 to
2 chopped green onions to the filling.

variations

shrimp panzerotti

see base recipe page 92

shrimp & basil panzerotti
Prepare the basic recipe, adding 2 tablespoons chopped fresh basil
to the filling.

shrimp & asparagus panzerotti
Prepare the basic recipe, adding 3 to 4 asparagus spears, steamed
and chopped to the filling.

shrimp & crab panzerotti
Prepare the basic recipe, replacing half the amount of shrimp with
an equal quantity of crabmeat.

shrimp & scallop panzerotti
Prepare the basic recipe, replacing half the amount of shrimp
with an equal quantity of small sautéed scallops.

shrimp & clam panzerotti
Prepare the basic recipe, replacing half the amount of shrimp with
an equal quantity of cooked clams.

variations

broccoli, asiago & pine nut calzones

see base recipe page 95

broccoli, parmesan & pine nut calzones
Prepare the basic recipe, replacing the Asiago with an equal quantity
of Parmesan.

spinach, asiago & pine nut calzones
Prepare the basic recipe, replacing the broccoli with 1 lb. cleaned,
stemmed, wilted, drained, and chopped spinach.

broccoli, asiago & garlic calzones
Prepare the basic recipe, omitting the pine nuts and adding
1 minced garlic clove.

broccoli & sun-dried tomato calzones
Prepare the basic recipe, omitting the pine nuts and adding
2 to 3 drained and chopped sun-dried tomatoes to the filling.

broccoli & mushroom calzones
Prepare the basic recipe, replacing the pine nuts with 1 cup sliced
button mushrooms that have been sautéed in 1 tablespoon butter
for 4 to 5 minutes to the filling.

mozzarella & ham stromboli

see base recipe page 96

mozzarella & basil pesto stromboli
Prepare the basic recipe, omitting ham slices. Spread each rectangle with 1/4 cup basil pesto (page 26). Replace mozzarella with 1 lb. bocconcini, torn into pieces and scattered over pesto.

mozzarella & pepperoni stromboli
Prepare the basic recipe, replacing the deli ham with an equal quantity of pepperoni.

three-cheese stromboli
Prepare the basic recipe, substituting 1/2 cup grated provolone and 1/2 cup grated fontina for 2 cups of the shredded mozzarella.

mozzarella & garlic stromboli
Prepare the basic recipe, spreading each rectangle of dough with 2 tablespoons roasted garlic purée before adding the cheese and ham.

mozzarella & tomato stromboli
Prepare the basic recipe, adding 1 thinly sliced fresh tomato to each stromboli before rolling it up.

variations

fontina & basil piadina

see base recipe page 98

fontina, broccoli & basil piadina
Prepare the basic recipe, adding 2 cups of steamed and chopped broccoli to the filling (1/4 cup broccoli per piadina).

fontina, tomato & basil piadina
Prepare the basic recipe, adding 1 to 2 tomato slices per piadina to the filling.

monterey jack & three-pepper piadina
Prepare the basic recipe, replacing the fontina with an equal quantity of grated Monterey Jack. Omit basil and season each piadina with freshly ground mixed peppercorns (black, white, and pink/red peppercorns).

fontina, ham & basil piadina
Prepare the basic recipe, adding 1 to 2 pieces of sliced deli ham per piadina.

fontina & spinach piadina with nutmeg
Prepare the basic recipe, omitting the basil. Add several leaves of fresh baby spinach and a pinch of nutmeg to each piadina.

crab & italian parsley calzones

see base recipe page 99

crab & chives calzones
Prepare the basic recipe, replacing the parsley with 2 tablespoons freshly chopped chives.

crab & sweet corn calzones
Prepare the basic recipe, adding 1/2 cup frozen corn to the filling mixture.

scallop & crab calzones
Prepare the basic recipe, using only 1/2 cup crabmeat and adding 1/2 cup cooked small scallops to the filling.

crab & thai basil calzones
Prepare the basic recipe, replacing the parsley with 2 tablespoons freshly chopped Thai basil.

crab & mussel calzones
Prepare the basic recipe, using only 3/4 cup crabmeat and 1/4 cup cooked small mussels.

variations

cheddar & bacon stuffed pizza

see base recipe page 101

cheddar & bacon stuffed pizza with herb crust
Prepare the basic recipe, adding 1 teaspoon Italian seasoning to the
flour mixture when making the dough.

havarti & parma ham stuffed pizza
Prepare the basic recipe, replacing the cheddar and Monterey Jack
with 1 cup grated Havarti, and replacing the bacon with an equal
quantity Parma ham, torn into strips.

cheddar, bacon & tomato stuffed pizza
Prepare the basic recipe, adding 1 chopped fresh tomato to the
filling mixture.

cheddar, bacon & pea stuffed pizza
Prepare the basic recipe, adding 1/2 cup frozen green peas to the
filling mixture.

provolone & pancetta stuffed pizza
Prepare the basic recipe, replacing the cheddar and the Monterey Jack
with 1 cup grated provolone, and the bacon with an equal quantity
pancetta, cubed and fried.

variations

sausage & mushroom calzones

see base recipe page 102

sausage, mushroom & pepper calzones
Prepare the basic recipe, adding 1 seeded and sliced green bell pepper
to the sausage and mushrooms.

sausage, mushroom & boursin calzones
Prepare the basic recipe, replacing the mozzarella with 8 oz.
Boursin cheese. Place 2 oz. Boursin in teaspoonfuls over the filling
before sealing the calzone.

sausage, mushroom & sun-dried tomato calzones
Prepare the basic recipe, adding 2 large roughly chopped sun-dried
tomatoes to the filling mixture with the pizza sauce.

turkey pepperoni & mushroom calzones
Prepare the basic recipe, omitting sausage. Place 3 to 4 slices of turkey
pepperoni over the dough before adding the mushrooms and sauce.

smoked tofu & mushroom calzones
Prepare the basic recipe, replacing the sausage with an equal quantity
of crumbled smoked tofu.

international pizzas

Wherever pizza is popular, people have experimented with new toppings. Using local ingredients and taste preferences as inspiration, many regions have developed their own specialty toppings. In some cases, as with the Hawaiian or Parisian pizzas, the name evolved in an entirely different location, where a recipe was developed to evoke the flavors associated with that distant place.

hawaiian pizza

see variations page 132

This pizza, made famous by its ham and pineapple topping, is especially popular with children.

1 recipe basic Neapolitan pizza crust (page 20)
1 recipe basic pizza sauce (page 25)
3 cups shredded mozzarella
1 cup pineapple pieces, drained and patted dry
1 cup diced cooked ham

Following the instructions on page 15, preheat a pizza stone in a 500°F (250°C) oven and roll out two 12-in. (30-cm.) circles of dough.

Lightly dust pizza peel with flour or cornmeal. Place one disc of pizza dough on peel and spread with half the pizza sauce, leaving a 1/2-in. (1-cm.) border.

Sprinkle with 1 1/2 cups grated mozzarella and top with 1/2 cup pineapple pieces and 1/2 cup ham. Gently shake pizza from the peel to the stone.

Bake 4 to 6 minutes, until cheese is melting and crust is puffy around edges and crispy on the bottom. Slide the peel back under the pizza to remove from oven. Repeat with the other pizza.

Makes two 12-in. (30-cm.) pizzas. Serves 6–8.

greek pizza

see variations page 133

Every bite of this pizza bursts with the classic flavors associated with Greece — feta, olives, and tomato.

1 recipe basic Neapolitan pizza crust (page 20)
1 tbsp. extra-virgin olive oil
1 small red onion, thinly sliced
1 garlic clove, minced

3 large fresh tomatoes, sliced
2 tsp. dried oregano, crumbled
1/2 cup sliced black olives
2 cups crumbled feta cheese

Following the instructions on page 15, preheat a pizza stone in a 500°F (250°C) oven and roll out two 12-in. (30-cm.) circles of dough.

To prepare the toppings, heat olive oil in skillet. Add onion and garlic. Cook for 2 to 3 minutes, until onion softens.

Lightly dust pizza peel with flour or cornmeal. Place one disc of pizza dough on peel and spread with half the onion mixture, leaving a 1/2-in. (1-cm.) border. Arrange half the tomato slices over the onions and sprinkle with 1 teaspoon oregano. Scatter 1/4 cup olives and 1 cup crumbled feta on top. Gently shake pizza from the peel to the stone.

Bake 4 to 6 minutes, until cheese is melting and crust is puffy around edges and crispy on the bottom. Slide the peel back under the pizza to remove from oven. Repeat with the other pizza.

Makes two 12-in. (30-cm.) pizzas. Serves 6–8.

parisian pizza

see variations page 134

With baby shrimp, fresh mushrooms, and sun-dried tomatoes, this pizza has a delightful medley of flavors and textures.

1 recipe basic Neapolitan pizza crust (page 20)
1 recipe basic pizza sauce (page 25)
3 cups shredded mozzarella
1 lb. cooked baby shrimp

1 cup sliced white mushrooms
6–8 sun-dried tomatoes, drained
   and coarsely chopped

Following the instructions on page 15, preheat a pizza stone in a 500°F (250°C) oven and roll out two 12-in. (30-cm.) circles of dough.

Lightly dust pizza peel with flour or cornmeal. Place one disc of pizza dough on peel and spread with half the pizza sauce.

Top with half the mozzarella, and distribute half the shrimp, mushrooms, and sun-dried tomatoes over the cheese. Gently shake pizza from the peel to the stone.

Bake 4 to 6 minutes, until cheese is melting and crust is puffy around edges and crispy on the bottom.

Slide the peel back under the pizza to remove from oven. Repeat with the other pizza.

Makes two 12-in. (30-cm.) pizzas. Serves 6–8.

brooklyn gourmet pizza

see variations page 135

The authentic Brooklyn Gourmet Pizza is baked in a brick oven and sliced into pieces big enough to fold in half. This is as close as you can get at home!

1 recipe basic Neapolitan pizza crust (page 20)
6 oz. skim-milk mozzarella, thinly sliced
6 oz. whole-milk mozzarella, thinly sliced
1 tsp. dried oregano, crumbled
freshly ground black pepper

1 cup canned tomatoes, drained
   and crushed
3 tbsp. extra-virgin olive oil
1/2 tsp. dried basil, or 6–8 fresh basil
   leaves, torn

Following the instructions on page 15, preheat a pizza stone in a 500°F (250°C) oven and roll out two 12-in. (30-cm.) circles of dough.

Lightly dust pizza peel with flour or cornmeal. Place one disc of pizza dough on peel and place half the mozzarella slices over dough, using a blend of whole-milk and skim-milk mozzarellas. Sprinkle with black pepper and oregano. Arrange 1/2 cup crushed tomatoes over seasonings, leaving spaces between tomato pieces. Drizzle with 1 1/2 tablespoons olive oil. Gently shake pizza from the peel to the stone.

Bake 4 to 6 minutes, until cheese is melting and crust is puffy around edges and crispy on the bottom. Slide the peel back under the pizza to remove from oven. Sprinkle with half of the basil. Repeat with the other pizza.

Makes two 12-in. (30-cm.) pizzas. Serves 6–8.

turkish pizza

see variations page 136

Inspired by the Turkish dish called Lahmacun, this pizza has the same luxurious ingredients—lamb scented with cinnamon, allspice, and cloves; tomatoes; and toasted pine nuts. The only real difference is this one is eaten flat instead of rolled or folded.

1 recipe basic Turkish pizza crust (page 15)
1 tbsp. oil
1/2 red onion, minced
1 lb. ground lamb
1 cup drained canned whole tomatoes
2 tbsp. tomato paste
1/2 cup finely chopped flat-leaf parsley
1/4 cup pine nuts, toasted

1/4 tsp. ground cinnamon
1/8 tsp. ground allspice
1/8 tsp. ground cloves
pinch of crushed red pepper flakes
1/2 tsp. salt
1/2 tsp. freshly ground black pepper
1 tbsp. fresh lemon juice
1/4 cup unsalted butter, melted

Following the instructions on page 15, let pizza dough rise while you make the lamb topping. To prepare the topping, heat 1 tablespoon oil in large skillet. Add minced onion and cook for 2 minutes, until translucent. Add lamb and cook until browned through. Stir in tomatoes, tomato paste, parsley, pine nuts, and seasonings. Simmer for 10 to 15 minutes, then add lemon juice. Preheat baking stone and oven to 450°F (230°C). Using a sharp knife, divide the dough into 16 egg-sized balls. Using rolling pin or fingers, stretch out each ball to form a 6-in. (15-cm.) disc, 1/8 in. (0.5 cm.) thick. Place on a lightly oiled cookie sheet and set aside for 10 minutes. Top each one with 2 tablespoons lamb mixture and drizzle with 1 teaspoon melted butter. Place Turkish pizzas on baking stone and bake for 8 to 10 minutes, until edge of crust is golden.

Makes 16 small pizzas. Serves 6–8.

montreal pizza

see variations page 137

Montreal is famous for its smoked meat, so it wasn't long before someone thought of putting it on pizza.

1 recipe basic Neapolitan pizza crust (page 20)
1 recipe basic pizza sauce (page 25)
3 cups shredded mozzarella
3 1/2 oz. Montreal smoked meat, sliced
    and cut into 1-in. (2-cm.) pieces

Following the instructions on page 15, preheat a pizza stone in a 500°F (250°C) oven and roll out two 12-in. (30-cm.) circles of dough.

Lightly dust pizza peel with flour or cornmeal. Place one disc of pizza dough on peel and spread with half the pizza sauce.

Sprinkle with 1 1/2 cups mozzarella and arrange half the smoked meat pieces over the cheese. Gently shake pizza from the peel to the stone.

Bake 5 to 7 minutes, until cheese is melting and crust is puffy around the edges and crispy on the bottom. Slide the peel back under the pizza to remove from oven. Repeat with the other pizza.

Makes two 12-in. (30-cm.) pizzas. Serves 6–8.

louisiana pizza

see variations page 138

With pieces of tender chicken, sweet corn kernels, and a chive and ricotta topping, this original pizza is extremely satisfying.

1 recipe basic Neapolitan pizza crust (page 20)
1 tbsp. unsalted butter
1 red bell pepper, diced
1 green bell pepper, diced
1/2 cup frozen or canned sweet corn kernels

1 cup diced cooked chicken breast
salt and freshly ground black pepper
1/2 cup ricotta cheese
2 tbsp. finely chopped fresh chives
1 recipe basic pizza sauce (page 25)

Following the instructions on page 15, preheat a pizza stone in a 500°F (250°C) oven and roll out two 12-in. (30-cm.) circles of dough.

To prepare the topping, melt butter over medium heat in large saucepan. Add diced peppers and cook 1 to 2 minutes until they begin to soften. Remove from heat and stir in corn and chicken. Season to taste. In small bowl, combine ricotta and chives. Lightly dust pizza peel with flour or cornmeal. Place one disc of pizza dough on peel and spread with half the pizza sauce. Spread half the chicken and corn mixture over the sauce and top with half the ricotta mixture. Gently shake pizza from the peel to the stone.

Bake 5 to 7 minutes, until cheese is melting and crust is puffy around edges and crispy on the bottom. Slide the peel back under the pizza to remove from oven. Repeat with the other pizza.

Makes two 12-in. (30-cm.) pizzas. Serves 6–8.

mexican pizza

see variations page 139

This spicy pizza will warm things up on a cool evening!

1 recipe basic Neapolitan pizza crust (page 20)
1 recipe basic pizza sauce (page 25)
3 cups shredded mozzarella
8 oz. spicy sausage, cooked, halved, and sliced
    into half-moon pieces
8 oz. pepperoni

1/2 yellow onion, sliced thin
1 small green pepper, seeded and
    sliced thin
1–2 hot chili peppers, seeded and finely
    chopped
1 fresh tomato, sliced

Following the instructions on page 15, preheat a pizza stone in a 500°F (250°C) oven and roll out two 12-in. (30-cm.) circles of dough.

Lightly dust pizza peel with flour or cornmeal. Place one disc of pizza dough on peel and spread with half the pizza sauce.

Sprinkle with half the mozzarella and arrange half the sausage, pepperoni, onion, peppers, and tomato on top. Gently shake pizza from the peel to the stone.

Bake 5 to 7 minutes, until cheese is melting and crust is puffy around edges and crispy on the bottom. Slide the peel back under the pizza to remove from oven. Repeat with the other pizza.

Makes two 12-in. (30-cm.) pizzas. Serves 6–8.

chicago deep-dish pizza

see variations page 140

The first deep-dish pizza is said to have been created at Chicago's Uno restaurant in the 1940s. It has been something of a phenomenon ever since.

1/3 recipe basic Chicago deep-dish pizza crust
    (page 22)
6 oz. mozzarella, sliced
2 cups cannned Italian plum tomatoes, drained
    and broken into chunks with wooden spoon
2 cloves garlic, minced

1/2 tsp. dried basil
1/2 tsp. dried oregano
salt and freshly ground black pepper
1/4 cup finely grated Parmesan
1–2 tbsp. extra-virgin olive oil

Following the instructions on page 15, roll the pizza dough into a ball.

Preheat oven to 475°F (240°C). Lightly dust dough ball with flour and using rolling pin, roll until disc is 11 in. (27 cm.) in diameter and 1/8 in. (0.5 cm.) thick. Lightly oil a 9 x 2-in. (23 x 5-cm.) round cake pan, and place dough in pan so that the edges are flush with the edge of the pan.

Arrange mozzarella slices over the bottom of the crust in a single layer. Place tomatoes over the cheese and sprinkle garlic and seasonings over tomatoes. Cover with grated Parmesan and drizzle oil in clockwise circle over top.

Bake for 35 to 40 minutes, until filling is hot and crust is puffy and golden brown.

Makes one 9-in. (23-cm.) deep-dish pizza. Serves 3–4

neapolitan pizza

see variations page 141

If you prepare the dough by hand and use San Marzano tomatoes for your sauce, your pizza will be as authentic as it can be without baking it in a wood-burning oven!

1 recipe basic Neapolitan pizza crust (page 20)
1 recipe basic pizza sauce, made with San
   Marzano tomatoes (page 25)

2 garlic cloves, thinly sliced
pinch of dried oregano
2 tbsp. extra-virgin olive oil

Following the instructions on page 15, preheat a pizza stone in a 500°F (250°C) oven and roll out two 12-in. (30-cm.) circles of dough.

Lightly dust pizza peel with flour. Place one disc of pizza dough on peel and spread with half the pizza sauce.

Arrange slices of 1 garlic clove over sauce and sprinkle with 1 tablespoon oregano.

Drizzle 1 tablespoon olive oil in clockwise motion over top of pizza. Gently shake pizza from the peel to the stone.

Bake 4 to 6 minutes, until crust is puffy around edges and crispy on the bottom. Slide the peel back under the pizza to remove from oven. Repeat with the other pizza.

Makes two 12-in. (30-cm.) pizzas. Serves 6–8.

variations

hawaiian pizza

see base recipe page 115

hawaiian pizza on whole-wheat crust
Prepare the basic recipe, replacing 1 cup bread flour with 1 cup whole-wheat flour.

hawaiian pizza with parma ham
Prepare the basic recipe, replacing the cooked ham with an equal quantity of Parma ham, thinly sliced and torn into strips.

hawaiian pizza with prosciutto
Prepare the basic recipe, replacing the cooked ham with an equal quantity of prosciutto, thinly sliced and torn into strips.

hawaiian pizza with figs
Prepare the basic recipe, adding 1 to 2 sliced fresh figs per pizza with the pineapple pieces.

hawaiian pizza with grapes
Prepare the basic recipe, adding 1/4 cup halved red grapes per pizza with the pineapple pieces.

greek pizza

see base recipe page 116

greek pizza with marinated tofu
Prepare the basic recipe, adding 1/2 cup marinated tofu cubes to each pizza with the olives and feta.

greek pizza with tzatziki
Prepare the basic recipe, spreading each pizza base with 2 to 3 tablespoons prepared tzatziki before adding the onions and other toppings.

greek pizza with kalamata olives
Prepare the basic recipe, replacing the black olives with an equal quantity of sliced kalamata olives.

greek pizza on gluten-free crust
Prepare the basic recipe, replacing the basic pan pizza crust with the Gluten-Free Pizza Crust (page 24).

greek pizza with lamb
Prepare the basic recipe, adding 1 cup ground lamb to the onion mixture. Cook until lamb is browned and cooked through.

variations

parisian pizza

see base recipe page 119

parisian pizza with brie
Prepare the basic recipe, replacing mozzarella with 8 oz. sliced Brie, divided between pizzas.

parisian pizza with escargots
Prepare the basic recipe, adding 10 oz. small French escargots per pizza. To prepare the snails, sauté in 3 tablespoons unsalted butter with 2 minced garlic cloves and season with salt and freshly ground black pepper.

parisian pizza with camembert
Prepare the basic recipe, replacing mozzarella with 8 oz. sliced Camembert, divided between pizzas.

parisian pizza with grape tomatoes
Prepare the basic recipe, adding 6 to 8 halved grape tomatoes per pizza, arranged over the cheese with the shrimp and mushrooms.

parisian pizza with arugula
Prepare the basic recipe, adding 4 oz. baby arugula leaves per pizza, arranged over the cheese with the shrimp and mushrooms.

variations

brooklyn gourmet pizza

see base recipe page 120

brooklyn gourmet sausage pizza
Prepare the basic recipe, replacing tomatoes with sausage pizza sauce (page 28).

brooklyn gourmet meat lovers' pizza
Prepare the basic recipe, adding 6 oz. sliced pepperoni and 8 oz. Italian
sausage (cooked, halved, and sliced into half-moon pieces), divided between
both pizzas over the cheese.

brooklyn gourmet vegetarian pizza
Prepare the basic recipe, adding 1 cup sliced mushrooms, 4 to 6 drained
and roughly chopped sun-dried tomatoes, 1/2 thinly sliced yellow onion, and
1/3 cup sliced black olives, divided between both pizzas over the tomatoes.

brooklyn gourmet pizza with ratatouille
Prepare the basic recipe, replacing tomatoes with 1 recipe ratatouille (page 29).

brooklyn gourmet salmon pizza
Prepare the basic recipe, omitting the crushed tomatoes and mozzarella.
Blend 1/4 cup pesto (page 26) with 1 cup ricotta. Spread ricotta topping
over crusts and bake according to instructions. Remove from oven and
top each pizza with 3 oz. smoked salmon, sliced thinly, and cut into strips.

variations

turkish pizza

see base recipe page 123

turkish pizza with spiced ground beef
Prepare the basic recipe, replacing ground lamb with an equal quantity
of lean ground beef.

turkish pizza with spiced ground pork
Prepare the basic recipe, replacing ground lamb with an equal
quantity of ground pork.

turkish pizza with spiced ground turkey
Prepare the basic recipe, replacing ground lamb with an equal quantity
of ground turkey.

turkish pizza with crumbled feta
Prepare the basic recipe, topping each pizza with 1 tablespoon
crumbled feta once they have been removed from the oven.

turkish pizza with spiced crumbled seitan
Prepare the basic recipe, replacing the ground lamb with an equal quantity
of crumbled seitan (wheat gluten).

variations

montreal pizza

see base recipe page 124

montreal pizza with hot peppers
Prepare the basic recipe, adding 2 oz. sliced marinated hot peppers
to each pizza with the smoked meat.

montreal pizza with rye crust
Prepare the basic recipe, replacing 1/2 cup all-purpose flour in the pizza
dough with 1/2 cup rye flour.

montreal pizza with pastrami
Prepare the basic recipe, replacing the Montreal smoked meat with
an equal quantity of pastrami.

montreal pizza with corned beef
Prepare the basic recipe, replacing the Montreal smoked meat
with an equal quantity of corned beef.

montreal pizza with mustard
Prepare the basic recipe, dotting each piece of smoked meat with
yellow mustard.

variations

louisiana pizza

see base recipe page 127

louisiana cheese & corn pizza
Prepare the basic recipe, omitting chicken.

louisiana pizza with gumbo
Prepare the basic recipe, replacing basic pizza sauce with an equal quantity of store-bought gumbo. Omit chicken mixture. Top gumbo with ricotta mixture.

louisiana pizza with okra
Prepare the basic recipe, adding 8 oz. drained and sliced canned okra to the chicken and corn mixture.

louisiana pizza with lobster
Prepare the basic recipe, replacing the chicken with an equal quantity of cooked lobster pieces.

louisiana pizza with button mushrooms
Prepare the basic recipe, adding 8 oz. diced button mushrooms to the peppers.

variations

mexican pizza

see base recipe page 128

mexican pizza on tortilla
Prepare the basic recipe, replacing the Neapolitan crust with 4 large store-bought or homemade tortillas (page 223). Divide sauce, cheese, and toppings in fourths and proceed with recipe.

tex-mex pizza
Prepare the basic recipe, replacing half the mozzarella with Monterey Jack cheese.

mexican pizza with cilantro
Prepare the basic recipe, adding 2 tablespoons chopped fresh cilantro to each pizza once it hs been removed from the oven.

mexican pizza with green salsa
Prepare the basic recipe, replacing the basic pizza sauce with 1/2 cup prepared green salsa per pizza.

mexican pizza with refried beans
Prepare the basic recipe, adding 1/4 cup refried beans per pizza.

variations

chicago deep-dish pizza

see base recipe page 130

vegetable deep-dish pizza
Prepare the basic recipe, arranging thin slices of 1/2 yellow onion, 4 oz. button mushrooms, and 1/2 green bell pepper over cheese before adding crushed tomatoes.

sausage deep-dish pizza
Prepare the basic recipe, replacing the crushed tomatoes with 1/2 recipe basic sausage pizza sauce (page 28).

four-cheese deep-dish pizza
Prepare the basic recipe, replacing half the mozzarella with 3 oz. sliced provolone. Add 1/4 cup grated fontina to top of pizza before adding Parmesan.

spinach deep-dish pizza
Prepare the basic recipe, replacing crushed tomatoes and seasonings with 1 lb. spinach, rinsed, stemmed, squeeze dried and chopped. Sauté 1 cup sliced mushrooms in 2 tbsp. extra-virgin olive oil. When mushrooms are beginning to brown, add 2 cloves minced garlic and cook for 2 minutes. Remove from heat, combine spinach and mushroom mixture. Season with salt and pepper. Proceed with recipe, or add 1/2 cup sliced mozzarella over the spinach mixture before sprinkling with Parmesan.

neapolitan pizza

see base recipe page 131

neapolitan pizza with anchovies
Prepare the basic recipe, adding 4 to 6 drained anchovy fillets per pizza. Arrange them like spokes from the center of the pizza to the edge.

neapolitan pizza with ricotta
Prepare the basic recipe, adding 4 to 5 teaspoons ricotta cheese in dollops over the sauce.

neapolitan pizza with sardines
Prepare the basic recipe, adding 4 to 6 drained sardine fillets per pizza. Arrange them like spokes from the center of the pizza to the edge.

neapolitan pizza with fresh basil
Prepare the basic recipe, adding 3 to 4 torn fresh basil leaves, per pizza. Scatter them over the sauce.

neapolitan pizza with herb crust
Prepare the basic recipe, adding 1/4 teaspoon Italian seasoning to the basic Neapolitan crust recipe with the flour.

fougasse, focaccia & european flatbreads

These irresistible and versatile flatbreads from all corners of Europe make delicious sandwiches, picnic foods, or accompaniments for hearty soups and stews. Try the crispy flatbreads with dips and cheese; enjoy the oatcakes and barley bread with butter and jam for breakfast.

classic fougasse

see variations page 160

Dotted with plump black olives, this fragrant flatbread is hard to resist.

1 tsp. active dry yeast
1 1/2 cups warm water
4 cups all-purpose flour
2 tbsp. extra-virgin olive oil

2 tsp. salt
1 1/2 cups pitted black olives
1/4 cup buckwheat flour
2 cups whole-wheat pastry flour

Sprinkle yeast over warm water in large bowl of standing mixer. Add 2 1/2 cups all-purpose flour and mix on slow speed for 1 minute. Cover bowl with plastic wrap and set aside for 30 minutes. Add olive oil, salt, olives, and buckwheat flour to yeast mixture and stir to combine. Mix in whole-wheat pastry flour. Add remaining all-purpose flour and switch to dough hook attachment. Knead for 4 to 5 minutes, until dough is smooth and soft. Place dough in lightly oiled bowl, rolling ball over to cover with light film of oil. Cover bowl with plastic wrap and place in warm spot to rise for 2 hours. Lightly oil 2 cookie sheets, 10 x 15 in. (25 x 40 cm.). Divide dough into 4 equal pieces. Cover remaining pieces while you work with first portion. Using your hands, stretch dough into wide oval shape, about 12 x 6 in. (30 x 15 cm.) and 1/2 in. (1 cm.) thick. Place on cookie sheet and cover with plastic wrap. Repeat with remaining pieces. Using sharp knife, make 3 cuts on each side in chevron pattern, leaving a 2-in. (2-cm.) border at top and bottom and a 1-in. (1-cm.) border on sides. Using your finger, pull open the cuts, leaving a bit of space dividing the 4 strips. Cover in plastic wrap and return to warm spot to rise for 30 minutes. Preheat oven to 400°F (200°C). Lightly glaze loaves with olive oil and bake for 20 minutes, until golden brown and puffy. Repeat with remaining two loaves.

Makes 4. Serves 10–12.

focaccia

see variations page 161

Easy to make, this beautiful fluffy flatbread is perfect for sandwiches or enjoying with soup.

1 tsp. sugar
2 1/4 tsp. active dry yeast (1 envelope)
1/3 cup warm water

2 cups all-purpose flour
2 tbsp. extra-virgin olive oil
1 tsp. sea salt

Dissolve sugar and yeast in warm water. Set aside for 10 minutes. In large bowl of standing mixer, combine yeast mixture with flour. Mix until all flour is incorporated. Change to dough hook attachment and knead for 1 to 2 minutes until dough is smooth.

Place dough in lightly oiled bowl, turning ball over to lightly coat with oil. Cover with a damp cloth and set aside in a warm spot for 30 to 40 minutes, until dough has doubled in size.

Preheat oven to 475°F (240°C). Place dough on lightly floured board and punch down once. Knead briefly, then shape the dough into a long flat rectangle with rounded corners, about 9 x 11 in. (23 x 28 cm.). Brush olive oil over surface and sprinkle with sea salt.

Place on cookie sheet lined with parchment paper or use pizza peel to transfer to preheated baking stone in bottom of oven. Bake for 10 to 15 minutes until lightly golden.

Makes 1. Serves 2–4.

ciabatta

see variations page 162

This Italian "slipper bread" is made with a starter dough, called "biga." Prepare the starter dough the day before you plan to bake your ciabatta.

biga
1/8 tsp. active dry yeast
2 tbsp. warm water
1/3 cup tepid water
1 cup bread flour

ciabatta
1/2 tsp. active dry yeast
2 tbsp. warm milk
2/3 cup tepid water
1 tbsp. olive oil
1 cup bread flour
1 cup all-purpose flour
1 1/2 tsp. salt

To prepare the biga, combine yeast and warm water in small bowl and set aside for 5 minutes. In a medium bowl, stir yeast mixture with tepid water and flour for 3 to 4 minutes, until smooth. Cover bowl with plastic wrap and let sit at room temperature for 12 to 24 hours. To prepare the ciabatta, combine yeast and warm milk in small bowl. Stir and set aside for 5 minutes. In large bowl of standing mixer, combine biga, yeast mixture, tepid water, oil, and flour. Mix until dough begins to come together. Add salt, change to dough hook attachment, and knead dough for 4 minutes. Ciabatta dough is supposed to be sticky. Do not add more flour! Transfer dough to a lightly oiled bowl and cover with plastic wrap. Place in a warm spot to rise for 2 hours, or until dough has doubled in size. Turn risen dough onto a lightly floured board or counter. Using a sharp knife, cut dough in half. Shape each piece

into a large oblong slipper shape, roughly 9–10 in. (23–25 cm.) long. Cover with damp paper towel and return to warm spot to rise for additional 2 hours, until dough has doubled again. Place baking stone or quarry tiles on bottom rack in electric oven or on bottom of gas oven. Preheat to 425°F (220°C) for 1 hour before baking. Lightly dust pizza peel with flour and set first loaf on peel. Gently shake ciabatta from the peel to the stone or tiles. Repeat quickly with second loaf. Bake for 20 minutes, until loaves are a light golden color. Slide pizza peel under loaves one at a time to remove from oven and transfer to wire rack to cool.

Makes 2. Serves 4–6.

hono

see variations page 163

This Swedish bread takes on many incarnations, but almost all involve the use of rye flour and anise seed.

1 tbsp. active dry yeast
1 1/2 cups warm water
1 tbsp. anise seeds
1 tbsp. fennel seeds
2 tbsp. grated orange zest
1/4 cup molasses

1/3 cup sugar
1 tbsp. salt
2 1/2 cups rye flour
2 tbsp. unsalted butter, softened
2 1/2–3 cups all-purpose flour
fine cornmeal, for dusting

Sprinkle yeast over warm water in large bowl of standing mixer and set aside for 10 minutes. Add anise and fennel seeds, orange zest, molasses, sugar, and salt; stir to blend. Add rye flour and butter; mix until all flour is incorporated. Add all-purpose flour and change to dough hook attachment. Knead for 4 to 5 minutes, and transfer dough to lightly oiled bowl, rolling to cover dough with thin film of oil. Cover bowl with plastic wrap and place in warm spot to rise for 2 hours, until dough has doubled in size. Knead by hand for 2 minutes. Cut dough in half. Lightly oil 2 large rectangular cookie sheets and dust with cornmeal. Using your hands, stretch dough into a wide oval shape. Place on cookie sheet and cover with clean damp kitchen towel. Repeat with second piece. Return to warm spot to rise for an additional hour. Preheat oven to 375°F (190°C). Using a sharp knife, make 3 to 4 diagonal slits in the top of each loaf. Bake for 30 to 35 minutes, until loaves are brown on top. Tap bottom crust; if it sounds hollow, the bread is done. Transfer to wire rack to cool.

Makes 2. Serves 8–10.

lefse

see variations page 164

Variations of this Norwegian potato flatbread abound — many families have their own favorite recipes. It is a common food at most Norwegian holidays.

4 cups potatoes, peeled, cooked, and finely
    mashed or run through a food mill or ricer
1/4 cup unsalted butter, cut into
    small squares

1/2 cup whipping cream
2 tsp. sugar
1 tsp. salt
1 1/2 cups all-purpose flour

While your potatoes are still warm, add butter and stir until it has completely melted and is well blended. Set aside to cool to room temperature. Add remaining ingredients, stirring until all the flour is incorporated and you have a smooth dough. Knead for 1 to 2 minutes. Using a 1/3 cup measuring cup, scoop 1/3 cup dough, then flatten into a 1-in.-thick (2-cm.) disc. Prepare all the patties and place them on a cookie sheet. Set aside for 5 minutes. Preheat electric skillet or lefse grill to 500°F (250°C). Lightly flour your rolling surface and rolling pin. Roll patty out to a 12-in. (30-cm.) round, although it doesn't have to be a perfect circle. Traditional lefse rolling pins are corrugated; their grooves prevent sticking. If your dough is sticking to the rolling pin, place a large sheet of plastic wrap over your patty and then roll over it. Peel off the plastic wrap before transferring to pan. Carefully slide a long metal spatula under lefse before you transfer, to make sure no spots are still sticking. Gently lift lefse from middle and transfer to hot pan or grill. Cook for 30 seconds per side, until golden brown spots begin to appear. Transfer cooked lefse to clean paper towel to cool. Lefse can be stacked and covered to cool. Lefse can be folded and stored in freezer for up to 6 months.

Makes 16–18. Serves 4–6.

crisp rye flatbread

see variations page 165

This crisp flatbread, known as "knekkerbrød" in Norway, became popular because it dries well and can be stored for long periods of time.

1 tbsp. active dry yeast	1 1/3 cups all-purpose flour
1 cup warm water	1 tsp. salt
1 1/3 cups rye flour	1/3 cup pumpernickel flour

Sprinkle yeast over warm water in a small bowl and set aside for 5 minutes. Combine flours and salt in large bowl of standing mixer. Incorporate yeast mixture on slow speed until dough begins to form.

Change to dough hook attachment and knead on slow speed, for 3 to 4 minutes, adding pumpernickel flour as necessary to make a smooth dough. Lightly flour board or counter with pumpernickel flour.

Turn dough onto surface and roll into a log. Slice log into 12 equal pieces and shape each piece into a ball. Place balls on cookie sheet, cover with a clean paper towel, and place in a warm spot to rise for 30 minutes.

Preheat oven to 425°F (220°C). Lightly oil 2 large rectangular cookie sheets. Using a rolling pin, roll out each ball to form a 4-in. (10-cm.) disc. Place discs on cookie sheets, prick surface with a fork, and bake for 8 to 10 minutes, until lightly browned. Transfer to wire rack to cool.

Makes 12. Serves 4–6.

bliny

see variations page 166

Bliny are Russian pancakes, made with a yeasted dough. They are traditionally served with a ground meat or sour cream filling; however, they have become quite popular in the West, where they are served with crème fraiche and smoked salmon or caviar.

1 cup all-purpose flour
1 tsp. salt
3/4 cup milk
1 1/4 tsp. active dry yeast

2 large eggs, separated
1/3 cup sour cream, crème fraiche, or whipping cream
canola oil, for greasing pan

Combine flour and salt in medium bowl. Warm 3/4 cup milk in saucepan. Remove from heat and sprinkle yeast over. Add egg yolks and sour cream to saucepan. Stir to blend. Slowly pour milk mixture into flour, stirring until batter is smooth. Cover bowl with plastic wrap and place in a warm spot to rise for 1 1/2 hours, until batter is foamy.

Beat egg whites in standing mixer with whisk attachment, until soft peaks form. Carefully fold egg whites into batter. Cover with plastic wrap and return to warm spot for additional 2 hours.

To cook bliny, lightly coat skillet with canola oil. Pour 1/6 cup batter for small bliny or 1/3 cup for large onto hot skillet and cook for 30 seconds to 1 minute per side, depending on the size of your bliny, until golden brown. Serve hot with topping of your choice.

Makes 10–12 small or 6 large bliny. Serves 2–3.

norwegian cracker bread

see variations page 167

This delicious cracker bread makes an excellent accompaniment for soups and dips.

1 cup whole-wheat flour
1 1/2–3 cups all-purpose flour
1 tsp. baking soda
1/4 tsp. salt

1 cup buttermilk
1/2 cup whipping cream
1/2 cup light corn syrup

In large bowl, blend whole-wheat flour, 1 1/2 cups all-purpose flour, baking soda, and salt. Stir in remaining ingredients until well incorporated into a smooth dough. Add up to 1 1/2 cups additional flour, 1/4 cup at a time, until dough stiffens.

Divide dough into 6 equal pieces. Place first ball on lightly floured board. Cover remaining pieces with moistened paper towel to prevent drying. Using rolling pin, roll dough to form a paper-thin rectangle with rounded corners, roughly 11 x 8 in. (28 x 20 cm.).

Preheat large electric skillet to 350°F (175°C). Transfer rolled dough to skillet and cook for 1 minute on each side. Repeat with 5 other pieces of dough. Preheat oven to 250°F (125°C).

Place cracker breads in a single layer on cookie sheets and bake for 10 minutes, or until crisp. To serve, break each piece into 4 crackers.

Makes 24. Serves 10–12.

oatcakes

see variations page 168

These Scottish oatcakes are served in wedges, known as "farls."

1 cup fine oatmeal (not rolled oats)
1/4 tsp. salt
1 tsp. salted butter, melted
1/3 boiling water

Set two large cast-iron skillets to warm over medium heat on stovetop.

Blend oatmeal and salt in medium bowl. Stir melted butter into 1/3 cup boiling water and pour into oatmeal mixture, until all dry ingredients are moistened. Add more boiling water if necessary, 1 tablespoonful at a time.

Lightly dust a wooden board or counter with oatmeal. Working quickly to prevent drying out, form 2 equal balls with the dough. Roll each one to a 6–8-in. (15–20-cm.) disc.

Using a sharp knife, cut into quarters and place the wedges in preheated skillet.

Cook over medium heat for 3 to 5 minutes, until wedges begin to brown. Flip wedges over and cook for an additional minute. Serve warm.

Makes 8. Serves 2–4.

barley breakfast bread

see variations page 169

This breakfast bread is easy to make — just make sure to soak the barley overnight for the most tender and flavorful results.

2 cups pearl barley	2 cups barley flour
2 cups buttermilk	1 tsp. baking soda
1 cup water	1 tsp. salt

Rinse barley and place in large bowl with buttermilk. Cover with plastic wrap and place in refrigerator to soak overnight.

In the morning, preheat oven to 350°F (175°C). Grease and flour an 8-in. (20-cm.) cast-iron skillet.

Stir water into barley mixture and, using handheld immersion blender or standing blender, reduce barley to fine particles.

Add remaining ingredients and pour the batter into skillet.

Bake for 45 to 50 minutes. Turn onto wire rack and let cool.

Makes one 8-in. (20-cm.) loaf. Serves 6–8.

variations

classic fougasse

see base recipe page 143

fougasse with sun-dried tomatoes
Prepare the basic recipe, replacing the olives with an equal quantity
of drained and chopped sun-dried tomatoes.

fougasse with walnuts
Prepare the basic recipe, replacing the olive oil with an equal quantity
of toasted walnut oil and replacing the olives with 1 cup coarsely
chopped walnuts.

whole-wheat fougasse
Prepare the basic recipe, replacing the buckwheat flour with an
equal quantity of whole-wheat pastry flour.

fougasse with chili peppers
Prepare the basic recipe, adding 2 seeded and chopped large jalapeño
chili peppers with the olives.

fougasse with rosemary
Prepare the basic recipe, adding 1 teaspoon dried and crumbled rosemary
with the olives. Crumbled rosemary can also be added to taste after glazing
the dough with olive oil.

variations

focaccia

see base recipe page 144

focaccia with summer vegetables
Prepare the basic recipe, spreading summer vegetable topping over dough prior to baking. To prepare topping, combine 2 tablespoons extra-virgin olive oil with 2 tablespoons balsamic vinegar. Brush mixture over 6 oz. zucchini and I red onion (in 1/4-in. / 0.5-cm. slices), and 1 quartered yellow bell pepper. Grill zucchini for 4 minutes per side; peppers and onions 6 minutes per side. Cool and slice peppers. Arrange vegetables over dough and top with 1/4 cup grated romano cheese.

focaccia with caramelized onions
Prepare the basic recipe, spreading caramelized onions over the dough prior to baking. To prepare the onions, cook 4 thinly sliced onions in 1/3 cup extra virgin olive oil in large skillet over low heat until soft and caramelized, about 30 minutes. Add 2 tablespoons balsamic vinegar and season with salt and pepper.

cheese focaccia
Prepare the basic recipe, omitting the sea salt and adding 1/4 cup grated romano cheese over the olive oil prior to baking.

focaccia with sage
Prepare the basic recipe, sprinkling 1 tablespoon fresh chopped sage over the focaccia with the sea salt.

variations

ciabatta

see base recipe page 146

cheese ciabatta
Prepare the basic recipe, adding 1/2 cup grated cheddar to the dough
before kneading.

ciabatta with sea salt
Prepare the basic recipe, dusting the tops of the loaves with 1 tablespoon
coarse sea salt before baking.

ciabatta with flax seeds
Prepare the basic recipe, adding 1/4 cup flax seeds to the dough
before kneading.

thyme ciabatta
Prepare the basic recipe, adding 1/4 teaspoon dried and crumbled thyme
to the dough before kneading.

ciabatta with smoked paprika
Prepare the basic recipe, adding 1/4 teaspoon smoked paprika to the
dough before kneading.

hono

see base recipe page 148

hono with celery seeds
Prepare the basic recipe, replacing the fennel seeds with an equal quantity of celery seeds.

hono with sunflower seeds
Prepare the basic recipe, replacing the fennel seeds with an equal quantity of sunflower seeds.

hono with barley
Prepare the basic recipe, replacing 1/2 cup all-purpose flour with 1/2 cup barley flour.

hono with cheese
Prepare the basic recipe, adding 1/4 cup finely grated Parmesan to the dough before kneading it.

hono with caraway seeds
Prepare the basic recipe, replacing the fennel seeds with an equal quantity of caraway seeds.

variations

lefse

see base recipe page 149

lefse with chives
Prepare the basic recipe, adding 2 tablespoons finely chopped fresh chives to the potato mixture before kneading.

cheese lefse
Prepare the basic recipe, adding 1/2 cup grated cheddar to the potato mixture before kneading.

lefse with corn
Prepare the basic recipe, adding 1/2 cup creamed corn to the potato mixture before kneading.

lefse with garlic
Prepare the basic recipe, adding 1 to 2 minced garlic cloves to the potato mixture before kneading.

variations

crisp rye flatbread

see base recipe page 151

crisp rye flatbread with fennel seeds
Prepare the basic recipe, adding 2 teaspoons fennel seeds with the flour.

crisp rye flatbread with flax seeds
Prepare the basic recipe, adding 2 teaspoons flax seeds with the flour.

crisp rye flatbread with cheese
Prepare the basic recipe, sprinkling 1 to 2 teaspoons finely grated Parmesan over each disc before baking them.

crisp rye flatbread with sesame seeds
Prepare the basic recipe, sprinkling 1/4 teaspoon sesame seeds over each disc before baking them.

crisp rye flatbread with herring
Prepare the basic recipe, garnishing each flatbread with a few pieces of pickled herring and a pinch of chopped fresh dill.

variations

bliny

see base recipe page 152

whole-wheat bliny
Prepare the basic recipe, replacing 1/2 cup all-purpose flour with
1/2 cup whole-wheat flour.

bliny with grated apple
Prepare the basic recipe, adding 1/2 cup peeled and grated apple
to the batter before cooking.

bliny with grated potato
Prepare the basic recipe, adding 1/2 cup peeled and grated potato
to the batter before cooking.

bliny with raisins
Prepare the basic recipe, adding 1/4 cup small golden raisins
to the batter before cooking.

buckwheat bliny
Prepare the basic recipe, replacing 1/2 cup all-purpose flour
with 1/2 cup buckwheat flour.

norwegian cracker bread

see base recipe page 155

norwegian cracker bread with fleur de sel
Prepare the basic recipe, sprinkling each piece with 1 tablespoon
fleur de sel before baking in oven.

norwegian cracker bread with flax seeds
Prepare the basic recipe, adding 2 teaspoons flax seeds to the flour mixture.

norwegian cracker bread with parmesan
Prepare the basic recipe, sprinkling each piece with 1 tablespoon finely
grated Parmesan before baking in oven.

norwegian cracker bread with gorgonzola
Prepare the basic recipe, serving each cracker with a wedge of Gorgonzola
topped with a slice of green apple.

norwegian cracker bread with oregano
Prepare the basic recipe, adding 1 teaspoon dried oregano to the
flour mixture.

variations

oatcakes

see base recipe page 156

oatcakes with strawberry jam
Prepare the basic recipe, spreading 1 tablespoon strawberry jam over each farl before serving.

oatcakes with aged cheddar
Prepare the basic recipe, topping each farl with a 1 oz. wedge of aged cheddar before serving.

oatcakes with marmite
Prepare the basic recipe, spreading each farl with 1/2 teaspoon marmite before serving.

oatcakes with onion chutney
Prepare the basic recipe, topping each farl with 1 teaspoon onion chutney before serving.

oatcakes with bran
Prepare the basic recipe, adding 1/4 cup bran flakes to the oatmeal mixture. Add more water to recipe if necessary.

barley breakfast bread

see base recipe page 159

barley bread with butter & jam
Prepare the basic recipe, spreading 1 teaspoon butter and 1 teaspoon raspberry jam over each slice before serving.

barley & spelt bread
Prepare the basic recipe, replacing 1/2 cup barley flour with 1/2 cup spelt flour.

barley & quinoa bread
Prepare the basic recipe, replacing 1/2 cup barley flour with 1/2 cup quinoa flour.

barley & oat bread
Prepare the basic recipe, replacing 1/2 cup barley flour with 1/2 cup fine oatmeal.

barley breakfast bread with dried apricots
Prepare the basic recipe, adding 1/2 cup coarsely chopped dried apricots to the dough with the remaining ingredients before baking.

indian &
african
flatbreads

This chapter contains every kind of texture

you could hope to find in flatbreads — from soft

naan to crispy papadum and chewy coconut

rotis. Experiment to see which ones pair the

best with your favorite spicy dishes.

naan

see variations page 188

This addictive flatbread is the perfect complement to any curry dish. Naan is traditionally baked by being slapped onto the wall of a tandoor oven.

1 1/2 tsp. active dry yeast
1 cup warm water
1/4 cup sugar
3 tbsp. whole milk
1 large egg, lightly beaten

2 tsp. salt
4 1/2 cups bread flour
1 garlic clove, peeled
1/4 cup unsalted butter

In large bowl of standing mixer, sprinkle yeast over warm water. Set aside for 10 minutes, until yeast becomes foamy. Add sugar, milk, egg, salt, and flour; mix well. Change to dough hook attachment and knead for 4 to 5 minutes, until dough is smooth. Place in lightly oiled bowl, rolling dough over to cover with thin film of oil. Cover bowl with a clean damp paper towel and place in a warm spot to rise for 1 hour, or until dough has doubled in size. Punch dough once to deflate. Using sharp knife, cut into 14 egg-sized pieces. Roll into 14 balls and place on lightly oiled cookie sheet. Cover with paper towel and return to warm spot for additional 30 minutes. Place baking stone or quarry tiles on bottom rack of oven and preheat to 450°F (230°C). Lightly flour pizza peel. Using fingers or rolling pin, shape dough into oblong shapes, roughly 6 x 4 in. (15 x 10 cm.). Place first naan on pizza peel and gently shake it onto baking stone. Repeat with as many naan as will fit on stone or tiles. Bake 8 to 10 minutes, until puffy with golden brown spots. While naan are baking, melt butter over low heat with garlic clove soaking in it. Brush hot naan with butter as they come out of oven. Repeat until all naan have been baked.

Makes 14. Serves 6–8.

chapatti

see variations page 189

This thin flatbread can be used to make wraps or to be served with curry or dhal.

1 cup whole-wheat flour
1 cup all-purpose flour
1 tsp. salt
2 tbsp. olive oil
3/4 cup hot water

Combine flours and salt in large bowl. Make a well in the middle and stir in olive oil
and just enough water to make a soft dough. Turn dough onto a lightly floured surface
and knead until it is smooth and elastic.

Use a sharp knife to cut the dough into 10 equal pieces. Shape each piece into a ball
and place on a cookie sheet. Set aside for 30 minutes.

Heat a large heavy skillet or *tava*. Lightly coat with oil. On a lightly floured board or
counter, roll dough out to a roughly 8-in. (20-cm.) round.

Place chapatti on hot pan and cook for 30 seconds per side, until brown spots appear.
Repeat with remaining balls of dough. Wrap the cooked chapatti with clean paper towel
to keep them soft as they cool. Serve warm or at room temperature.

Makes 10. Serves 4–5.

papadum

see variations page 190

These crisp lentil-based flatbreads must dry for several days before they are fried, toasted, or broiled.

1 oz. mung lentils, finely ground
1/4 tsp. freshly ground black pepper
1/4 tsp. finely ground red chili pepper
salt
1/3 cup water

Place all ingredients in a saucepan and cook over medium heat for 3 minutes, until water has been completely absorbed. Cool to room temperature. Divide dough into 8 equal portions and shape into balls. Place a sheet of plastic wrap or parchment paper on a board. Place a dough ball on top and cover with another sheet. Roll the ball into a paper-thin 4-in. (10-cm.) round. Repeat with the other balls.

Place rounds on a wire rack to dry for 24 hours at room temperature or outside in hot summer sun. Turn papadum over and repeat for 3 more days. Store dried papadum in an airtight container.

To serve papadum, heat several inches of canola oil in a deep skillet. Use tongs to place papadum in hot oil. Cook for 10 seconds, remove, and place on wire rack to drain and cool. Alternatively, toast in toaster oven or cook for a few seconds in oven broiler.

Makes 8. Serves 2–3.

sri lankan coconut roti

see variations page 191

These sweet flatbreads make a pleasing addition to a spicy meal.

2 cups all-purpose flour
1/2 tsp. salt
1 1/2 cups shredded coconut
1/4 cup boiling water
1 tbsp. unsalted butter

Combine flour, salt, and coconut in large bowl. Add enough boiling water to make a soft dough that is not sticky. Turn dough onto lightly floured surface and knead for 5 minutes.

Divide dough into 12 egg-sized pieces, then flatten each one into a 3-in. (8-cm.) disc. Place disc between 2 sheets of plastic wrap or parchment paper and roll out to 1/12-in. (4-cm.) thickness.

Preheat oven to 275°F (140°C). Preheat large skillet over high heat. When skillet is very hot, peel roti off paper and place in skillet. Cook for 1 minute per side, until roti begins to brown.

Place on ovenproof plate in oven to keep warm until serving time. Repeat with other roti.

Makes 12. Serves 4–6.

parathi

see variations page 192

This fried flatbread is folded twice; the four layers result in a delightfully flaky texture.

2 cups whole-wheat pastry flour
1 1/2 cups all-purpose flour
1 tsp. sea salt

3 tbsp. canola oil
1 cup warm water
1/2 cup unsalted butter, melted

Combine the whole-wheat flour, 1 cup all-purpose flour, and salt in the large bowl of standing mixer. Make a well in the center of the flour mixture and pour in the canola oil. Rub oil into the flour by picking up a portion of the flour and oil with your right hand, picking up some flour with your left hand, and sliding your left hand from palm to fingers over your right hand. Repeat until all the flour is moistened and no lumps of oil remain. Add warm water, mixing on slow speed until dough forms. Change to dough hook and knead dough for 5 to 6 minutes, until it is very soft and smooth. Cover bowl with plastic wrap and place in a warm spot for 30 minutes. Turn dough onto a lightly floured board or counter. Knead dough briefly by hand, 1 to 2 minutes, then divide in half. Using your hands, roll each piece into a log. With a sharp knife, cut each log into 8 equal pieces and shape each into a small ball. Dust balls with remaining 1/2 cup all-purpose flour, place in bowl, and cover with a clean damp kitchen cloth to prevent drying. Place one ball of dough on lightly floured board. Flatten into a disc, dust both sides with flour, then roll out to a 5-in. (12-cm.) round. Brush the top with melted butter and fold in half. Again, glaze the top of the half-moon shape with melted butter and fold in half. Lightly dust both sides of the triangular patty with

flour and roll out until you have a 7-in. (18-cm.) triangle. Repeat process with the other 15 balls of dough. Preheat oven to 275°F (140°C). Heat large cast-iron skillet on a hot burner. When skillet is hot, cook first triangle of dough for 2 minutes, until golden brown spots appear on bottom. Flip and cook for 15 to 20 seconds. Brush with melted butter, flip and cook for 30 seconds. Brush second side and repeat. Transfer parathi to ovenproof dish and place in oven to keep warm. Repeat with remaining triangles of dough.

Makes 16. Serves 6–8.

dosa

see variations page 193

Dosai, traditionally served as breakfast food, are made from a batter of split, skinned urad beans that have soaked overnight.

3/4 cup split and skinned urad beans
3 1/2 cups water, plus more for soaking
2 cups rice flour

1 tsp. salt
1 tbsp. canola oil

Place beans in small bowl. Cover with water and leave to soak 10 to 12 hours at room temperature. Drain the beans and purée in blender, adding up to 1 cup water as necessary to make a smooth paste. In small saucepan over low heat, warm 1/2 cup water. Add 1 tablespoon rice flour and whisk until it thickens. Remove from heat and set aside. Combine bean purée, salt, remaining rice flour, and remaining 2 cups water in large bowl of standing mixer. Mix on medium speed until batter is smooth and thin. Reduce speed to slow and incorporate reserved rice flour mixture. When batter is smooth, cover with plastic wrap and set aside for 6 to 12 hours.

Preheat oven to 275°F (140°C). Lightly oil and preheat large heavy-bottomed skillet. When pan is hot, pour 1/2 cup batter onto center of pan, tilting the pan in an up-and-down, side-to-side motion to help spread the batter to a thin 8–10-in. (20–25-cm.) round. Cook for 1 to 2 minutes per side, until dosa is golden brown and crispy around the edges. Place cooked dosa on an ovenproof plate and place in oven to keep warm while you prepare the rest of the batter.

Make 16–18. Serves 5–6.

injera

see variations page 194

This spongy Ethiopian flatbread is made from a batter that has fermented for at least 24 hours. Injera is the ultimate finger food; it is placed on the plate beneath several portions of various stews and is used to scoop up mouthfuls.

1 tsp. active dry yeast
3 cups warm water
2 cups teff flour

In small bowl, sprinkle yeast over 1/2 cup warm water. Set aside for 5 minutes. Place flour in large bowl of standing mixer. Add 2 1/2 cups warm water and stir to combine. Stir in yeast mixture. Cover bowl with plastic wrap and leave to ferment at room temperature for 24 to 72 hours.

Preheat large heavy-bottomed skillet. When skillet is hot, pour 1/2 cup batter onto center of pan, tilting the pan in an up-and-down, side-to-side motion to help spread the batter to a thin 10–12-in. (25–30-cm.) round. Unlike pancakes, injera only cook on one side.

Cook for 2 minutes over low heat, until surface is spongy and cratered and edges are curling up slightly. Transfer to plate to cool.

Makes 6–8. Serves 3–4.

chickpea flatbread

see variations page 195

This healthy flatbread is the perfect addition to a tapas spread.

2 tsp. active dry yeast	1 tbsp. salt
1 cup warm water	1 cup (8 oz.) chickpeas, drained and mashed
1 tbsp. honey	1 1/2 tsp. cumin seeds, slightly crushed
3 1/2 cups bread flour	1 1/2 tsp. coriander seeds, slightly crushed

In small bowl, sprinkle yeast over 1/2 cup warm water. Stir in honey. Set aside for 5 minutes. In large bowl of standing mixer, combine 2 cups flour and salt. Add yeast mixture and mix on slow speed until incorporated. Add remaining flour, mashed chickpeas, and seeds. Stir to combine. Add up to 1/2 cup more warm water and up to 1/2 cup more bread flour to make a smooth, moist dough. Change to dough hook attachment and knead for 4 to 5 minutes. Place dough in lightly oiled bowl, rolling dough over to cover with a thin film of oil. Cover bowl with plastic wrap and place in a warm spot to rise for 1 hour, or until doubled in size.

Place baking stone on bottom rack and preheat oven to 450°F (230°C). Punch dough down once to deflate, then divide into 5 equal pieces. Lightly flour pizza peel. Using fingers or rolling pin, shape dough into oblong shapes, roughly 1/4 in. (0.5 cm.) thick. Place first flatbread on pizza peel and gently shake it onto baking stone.

Bake 2 to 3 flatbreads at a time, for 4 to 5 minutes, until they are puffy and golden brown. Transfer to wire rack to cool slightly.

Makes 5. Serves 6–8.

spicy moroccan flatbread with olives

see variations page 196

This flatbread, made without yeast, is covered with an exquisite blend of seasonings.

1 cup, plus 1 1/2 tbsp. all-purpose
    flour
2 tsp. sugar
1 tsp. salt
1/4 tsp. freshly ground black pepper
10 Moroccan olives, drained, pitted, and
    coarsely chopped

1 tbsp. extra-virgin olive oil, plus more
    for glazing
1/2 cup water
1/4 tsp. salt
1/2 tsp. garlic powder
1/4 tsp. curry powder
1/4 tsp. ground cumin

In large bowl of standing mixer, combine flour, sugar, salt, pepper, and chopped olives. Stir in 1 tablespoon of olive oil. Add water and mix until dough forms a ball. Change to dough hook attachment and knead for 1 to 2 minutes, until dough is smooth. Cover bowl with plastic wrap and refrigerate for 1 hour. To prepare spice blend, combine the remaining ingredients in a small bowl. Set aside. Preheat oven to 400°F (200°C) and line a large rectangular cookie sheet with parchment paper. Lightly wipe paper with olive oil. Turn dough onto lightly floured board or counter. Using rolling pin, roll dough into a paper-thin oblong shape. Carefully transfer dough to cookie sheet. Lightly glaze flatbread with olive oil and sprinkle with spice blend. Place cookie sheet on rack in middle of oven and bake for 20 minutes, until flatbread is golden brown. Transfer to wire rack to cool. Break into pieces to serve.

Makes 1. Serves 4–5 as an appetizer.

cardamom flatbread

see variations page 197

Cardamom is the spice made from grinding the aromatic seeds from a plant in the ginger family. It lends a delicate flavor to this sweet stuffed flatbread.

dough
1 cup all-purpose flour
pinch of salt
1 1/2 tbsp. canola oil, warmed
1/4 cup water

filling
1/4 cup chickpea flour
1 tsp. canola oil
1 cup brown sugar
1 tbsp. poppy seeds
1/4 tsp. cardamom
pinch of nutmeg
2 tbsp. unsalted butter, melted

To prepare dough, combine flour, salt, and 1 tablespoon oil in large bowl of standing mixer. Add just enough water to form stiff dough. Change to dough hook attachment and knead for 2 minutes. Set aside for 10 minutes. Knead again, adding remaining tablespoon of oil to soften dough. Form dough into balls the size of small peach. To prepare filling, cook chickpea flour in 1 teaspoon oil until golden. Combine chickpea flour mixture with brown sugar, poppy seeds, cardamom, and nutmeg. Knead by hand and form walnut-sized balls. Flatten 2 dough balls into discs. Flatten a ball of filling and sandwich it between the discs. Using rolling pin, roll sandwich into thin disc, 5–6 in. (12–15 cm.) wide. Repeat with rest of dough and filling. Preheat oven to 275°F (140°C). Heat a large cast-iron or nonstick skillet over medium-high heat. Cook flatbread for 2 minutes, or until bottom layer browns. Brush top layer with melted butter and cook for another minute. Repeat until both sides are golden brown. Repeat until all dough is used up. Serve warm.

Makes 3–4. Serves 3–4.

variations

naan

see base recipe page 171

naan with cumin
Prepare the basic recipe, adding 1 teaspoon ground cumin with the flour. Sprinkle a pinch of cumin seeds over each naan before baking.

naan with nigella seeds
Prepare the basic recipe, sprinkling each naan with a pinch of nigella seeds before baking.

garlic naan
Prepare the basic recipe, adding 1 minced garlic clove with the flour.

naan with ghee
Prepare the basic recipe, replacing the unsalted butter with an equal quantity of ghee.

chapatti

see base recipe page 172

chapatti with ghee
Prepare the basic recipe, brushing each chapatti with ghee before serving.

millet chapatti
Prepare the basic recipe, replacing 1/2 cup whole-wheat flour with 1/2 cup millet flour.

corn flour chapatti
Prepare the basic recipe, replacing 1/2 cup whole-wheat flour with 1/2 cup fine cornmeal.

whole-wheat chapatti
Prepare the basic recipe, replacing the all-purpose flour with an equal quantity of whole-wheat flour.

variations

papadum

see base recipe page 175

papadum with pink peppercorns
Prepare the basic recipe, adding 1/4 teaspoon crushed pink peppercorns.

papadum with cayenne
Prepare the basic recipe, adding a pinch of cayenne pepper.

papadum with cumin
Prepare the basic recipe, adding 1/4 teaspoon ground cumin.

papadum with garlic
Prepare the basic recipe, adding 1/4 teaspoon garlic powder.

sri lankan coconut roti

see base recipe page 176

sri lankan coconut roti with raspberry jam
Prepare the basic recipe, spreading each roti with 1 to 2 tablespoons
raspberry jam before serving.

sri lankan coconut roti with honey
Prepare the basic recipe, spreading each roti with 1 tablespoon honey
before serving.

sri lankan coconut roti with treacle
Prepare the basic recipe, spreading each roti with 1 tablespoon treacle
before serving.

sri lankan coconut with banana
Prepare the basic recipe, topping each roti with several slices
of fresh banana.

variations

parathi

see base recipe page 178

parathi with potatoes
Prepare the basic recipe, topping each paratha with 1 to 2 tablespoons prepared potato curry.

parathi with egg
Prepare the basic recipe, topping each paratha with 1 to 2 tablespoons scrambled egg.

parathi with chutney
Prepare the basic recipe, topping each paratha with 1 to 2 tablespoons chutney.

parathi with pomegranate seeds
Prepare the basic recipe, topping each paratha with 1 tablespoon pomegranate seeds.

variations

dosa

see base recipe page 180

semolina dosa
Prepare the basic recipe, replacing 1/2 cup rice flour with 1/2 cup fine semolina flour.

dosa with omelet
Prepare the basic recipe, placing 2 oz. omelet in the middle of each dosa. Fold the top and bottom over the filling and roll the dosa up, as you would a burrito.

dosa with ghee
Prepare the basic recipe, brushing each dosa with 1 tablespoon ghee.

dosa with onions
Prepare the basic recipe, placing 1/4 cup caramelized onions in the middle of each dosa. Fold the top and bottom over the filling and roll the dosa up, as you would a burrito.

variations

injera

see base recipe page 181

wheat injera
Prepare the basic recipe, replacing teff flour with an equal quantity of
all-purpose flour. Increase yeast to 2 teaspoons. Reduce standing time
to 2 to 3 hours.

corn injera
Prepare the basic recipe, replacing 1/2 cup teff flour with 1/2 cup
fine cornmeal.

barley injera
Prepare the basic recipe, replacing 1/2 cup teff flour with 1/2 cup
barley flour.

rice injera
Prepare the basic recipe, replacing 1/2 cup teff flour with 1/2 cup rice flour.

variations

chickpea flatbread

see base recipe page 183

chickpea flatbread with saffron
Prepare the basic recipe, adding 1/3 teaspoon saffron threads steeped in 1/4 cup warm water for 10 minutes with the mashed chickpeas. Omit cumin and coriander seeds.

chickpea flatbread with smoked paprika
Prepare the basic recipe, adding 1/4 teaspoon smoked paprika with the other spices.

chickpea flatbread with mint
Prepare the basic recipe, adding 1/2 teaspoon dried mint with the other spices.

chickpea flatbread with ground pomegranate seeds
Prepare the basic recipe, adding 1 teaspoon ground pomegranate seeds with the other seeds.

variations

spicy moroccan flatbread with olives

see base recipe page 184

spicy moroccan flatbread with sun-dried tomatoes
Prepare the basic recipe, replacing the olives with 1/4 cup drained
and chopped sun-dried tomatoes.

spicy moroccan flatbread with figs
Prepare the basic recipe, replacing the olives with 1/4 cup chopped
dried figs.

spicy moroccan flatbread with currants
Prepare the basic recipe, replacing the olives with 1/4 cup dried currants.

spicy moroccan flatbread with peppers
Prepare the basic recipe, replacing the olives with 1/4 cup chopped
roasted red peppers.

cardamom flatbread

see base recipe page 187

cardamom & cinnamon flatbread
Prepare the basic recipe, adding 1/4 teaspoon ground cinnamon with the other spices.

cardamom & allspice flatbread
Prepare the basic recipe, adding a pinch of ground allspice with the other spices.

cardamom chocolate flatbread
Prepare the basic recipe, adding 2 tablespoons unsweetened cocoa powder with the spices.

cardamom walnut flatbread
Prepare the basic recipe, adding 1/4 cup finely chopped walnuts to the filling.

flatbreads & hearth breads of the middle east

The flatbreads in this chapter are as diverse as the countries they originate from. Whether you want something soft and pliable or crispy and covered in seeds, you are sure to find the perfect flatbread to serve with your next Middle Eastern feast.

matzoh

see variations page 214

For matzoh to be considered kosher for Passover, it must finish baking within 18 minutes of the water having come into contact with the grain. This ensures that no fermentation has occurred.

2 cups matzoh meal
1/2 tsp. kosher salt
1 1/2 cups kosher spring water

Preheat oven to 450°F (230°C). In a large bowl, combine matzoh meal and salt. Pour in water and stir until a dough forms. Working quickly, turn dough onto a surface lightly floured with matzoh meal and knead for 3 to 4 minutes. Cut the dough into 8 equal pieces.

Working with one piece at a time, roll dough as thin as possible between 2 sheets of parchment paper. Peel off top layer of parchment paper and transfer other piece to large rectangular cookie sheet. Cut dough into four 3-in. (8-cm.) squares. Prick surface of dough with fork or pastry docker.

Place in preheated oven and bake for 3 to 4 minutes, until golden and crisp. Transfer to wire rack to cool and dry. Repeat with remaining dough.

To meet time constraints, ensure that at least two people are preparing the matzohs. Bake up to 4 pieces of dough at once, using 4 separate baking sheets.

Makes 32 matzoh squares

manakish

see variations page 215

This Lebanese specialty has become popular around the world. Topped with a delectable blend of thyme and sesame seeds, zahtar flatbread works well with other mezze dishes.

1 1/4 tsp. active dry yeast
1 1/2 cups all-purpose flour
1/2 cup warm water
1/2 tsp. salt

1 cup dried thyme
1 cup ground sumac
1 tbsp. sesame seeds
3 tbsp. extra-virgin olive oil

In a medium bowl, combine yeast, 1 tablespoon flour, and 1/4 cup warm water. Stir and set aside for 10 minutes, until mixture becomes foamy. In large bowl of standing mixer, combine salt and 3/4 cup flour. Add yeast mixture and remaining water. Mix until well incorporated. Add remaining flour and mix until dough begins to pull away from sides of bowl. Change to dough hook attachment and knead for 4 to 5 minutes, until dough is smooth and elastic. Shape dough into a ball, dust with flour, place in bowl, and cover with plastic wrap. Place bowl in warm spot to rise for 1 1/2 hours, until dough has doubled in size. To prepare zahtar spice blend, combine the thyme, sumac, and sesame seeds in medium bowl. Stir in olive oil to form a paste. Place baking stone on lowest rack in oven and preheat to 350°F (175°C). Turn dough onto lightly floured surface and roll out to form an oblong shape, roughly 12 x 8 in. (30 x 20 cm.). Spread zahtar spice blend over flatbread. Lightly flour pizza peel. Place flatbread on pizza peel and gently shake it onto baking stone. Bake for 3 to 4 minutes, or until flatbread is golden brown and crispy around the edges. Serve warm.

Makes 1. Serves 2–3.

sangak

see variations page 216

In Iran, sangak is baked in a large oven over hot stones, giving it a unique texture.
This version is divided in smaller pieces to fit into home ovens.

1 tbsp. active dry yeast
2 1/2 cups warm water
1 1/2 tsp. salt

3 cups whole-wheat flour
1 cup all-purpose flour
12 tsp. sesame seeds

In a large bowl of standing mixer, sprinkle the yeast over 1/2 cup warm water. Set aside for
5 minutes. Stir in salt and 1 1/2 cups warm water, and set aside for 10 more minutes. Add
flour, 1 cup at a time, and remaining water. Mix on low speed until dough is smooth. Place
dough in lightly oiled bowl, cover with a damp paper towel, and place in a warm spot to rise
for 3 hours, until dough has doubled in size. Place baking stone on bottom rack and preheat
oven to 500°F (250°C). Return dough to large bowl of standing mixer, and change to the
dough hook attachment. Knead for 5 to 6 minutes. Using a sharp knife, divide the dough
into 6 equal pieces. With fingers or rolling pin, stretch out dough to an oblong shape,
1/2 in. (1 cm.) thick. Lightly flour pizza peel. Place first flatbread on pizza peel. Dimple the
surface with damp fingertips, sprinkle with 2 teaspoon sesame seeds, and gently shake it
onto baking stone. Bake for 3 to 4 minutes, pressing the loaf down with the pizza peel to
flatten it after the first minute. Slide pizza peel under the flatbread to remove from oven.
Using tongs, flip the flatbread over and return to baking stone to bake for 2 minutes longer.
Transfer to a wire rack to cool. Repeat with remaining loaves.

Makes 6. Serves 10–12.

barbari

see variations page 217

This long flatbread is known for its distinctive ridges.

1/4 cup warm water
2 tsp. active dry yeast
5 cups all-purpose flour
1 1/2 tsp. salt
3 tbsp. sugar

3 tbsp. unsalted butter, melted
2 cups warm water
2 tbsp. milk
1/4 cup sesame seeds

In small bowl, sprinkle yeast over 1/4 cup warm water. Stir and set aside for 5 minutes, until dissolved. Place flour in large bowl of standing mixer. Make well in center of flour and pour in yeast mixture, salt, sugar, melted butter, and water. Blend on slow speed. When flour is completely incorporated, change to dough hook attachment. Knead for 4 to 5 minutes, until dough is smooth and elastic. Shape dough into ball and place in lightly oiled bowl, rolling dough over to cover with thin film of oil. Cover with clean, damp paper towel and place in warm spot to rise for 1 hour, until doubled in size. Place baking stone on lower rack and preheat oven to 350°F (175°C). Punch dough down once to deflate. Using sharp knife, cut dough into 4 equal pieces. Shape each piece into ball. Place on lightly floured board, dust with flour, cover, and return to warm spot for additional 20 minutes. Using fingers or rolling pin, stretch out each piece to form oblong shape, roughly 12 x 6 in. (30 x 15 cm.). Using the side of one thumb, make ridges from one end of loaf to other, lengthwise, leaving a 1-in. (2-cm.) border on all sides and 1 in. (2 cm.) between each ridge. Brush loaf with 1/2 tablespoon

milk and sprinkle with 1 tablespoon sesame seeds. Prepare remaining three flatbreads and set aside for 15 minutes. Lightly flour pizza peel. Gently shake one flatbread from peel onto baking stone. Bake 2 at a time if space allows. Bake for 20 to 25 minutes, or until flatbread is puffy and golden brown. Transfer to wire rack to cool.

Makes 4. Serves 8–10.

pita

see variations page 218

This popular flatbread, also known as pocket bread, is used to make stuffed sandwiches. If any of your pita breads do not puff up sufficiently, use them for making pita chips.

1 tsp. active dry yeast
1/4 cup warm water
1/2 tbsp. extra-virgin olive oil
1/2 tbsp. honey

3/4 cup tepid water
1 cup whole-wheat flour
1 1/2 cups all-purpose flour
1 tsp. salt

In small bowl, sprinkle yeast over 1/4 cup warm water. Stir and set aside for 5 minutes, until yeast has dissolved. Combine oil, honey, and tepid water in large bowl. Combine flours and salt in large measuring cup. With mixer on slow, incorporate flour mixture and yeast mixture into oil and honey mixture. Cover bowl with clean paper towel and set aside for 20 minutes. Sprinkle salt over dough, change to dough hook attachment, and knead for 4 to 5 minutes, until dough is smooth and elastic. Turn dough into clean bowl, cover, and place in warm spot to rise for 1 1/2 to 2 hours, until dough has doubled in size. Turn dough onto lightly floured surface. Using sharp knife, cut into 8 equal pieces. Shape each piece into ball, dust with flour, cover with clean damp paper towel, and set aside for 30 minutes. Place baking stone on lowest rack and preheat oven to 500°F (250°C). Using rolling pin, roll out each ball to 6-in. (15-cm.) disc, 1/4 in. (0.5 cm.) thick. Carefully place sheet of aluminium foil over baking stone to diffuse heat slightly. Lightly flour pizza peel and gently shake pita breads from peel onto foil-covered stone. Bake for 5 minutes, until pitas are golden and puffed up. Place large rectangle of aluminum foil on wire rack. Transfer baked pitas to aluminum foil and carefully wrap them up.

Makes 8. Serves 3–4.

lavash

see variations page 219

Lavash is a paper-thin Armenian flatbread that is soft and supple when warm and dry and brittle when cooled.

1 tbsp. honey	2 1/2 cups unbleached
1 1/2 cups warm water	bread flour
1/2 tsp. active dry yeast	1 tsp. salt

In a small bowl, combine honey and warm water. Sprinkle yeast over water, stir, and set aside for 5 minutes, until dissolved. Place 2 cups flour in large bowl of standing mixer. Make a well in the middle of the flour and pour in the yeast mixture. Mix on slow speed for 1 minute. Add salt and remaining flour. If dough is still soft, add up to 1/2 cup more flour until you have a stiff dough. Change to dough hook attachment. Knead for 4 to 5 minutes, until dough is smooth and elastic. Turn dough into a clean bowl, cover with plastic wrap, and place in a warm spot to rise for 3 hours, until dough has doubled in size.

Punch dough once to deflate, then set aside for 10 minutes. Place baking stone or tiles on lowest rack and preheat oven to 450°F (230°C). Turn dough onto lightly floured board or counter, and pat into a large rectangle. Using a sharp knife, cut dough into 8 equal square-shaped pieces. Keeping remaining pieces covered, roll first square out to a paper-thin rectangle, roughly 12 x 10 in. (30 x 25 cm.). Prick holes in dough with fork. Lightly flour pizza peel and gently transfer first piece of lavash to baking stone. Bake for 2 to 3 minutes, until pale brown. Transfer to wire rack to cool. Repeat with remaining pieces.

Makes 8. Serves 8–10.

garlic hearth bread

see variations page 220

This easy and aromatic hearth bread will satisfy the deepest craving for roasted garlic.

1 head fresh garlic, papery top removed
1 tsp. plus 2 tbsp. extra-virgin olive oil
3 1/2 cups bread flour
2 tsp. quick-rise yeast

2 tsp. salt
5 tbsp. extra-virgin olive oil
1 1/3 cups warm water

To prepare roasted garlic, preheat oven to 375°F (190°C). Place head of garlic on large square of aluminum foil. Drizzle oil over garlic and wrap foil around garlic, twisting at top to make neat parcel. Place in oven for 45 minutes. Let cool, then squeeze garlic out of skins into small bowl. Mash garlic and stir in 2 tablespoons oil, until smooth. To prepare hearth bread, place baking stone or tiles on middle rack and preheat oven to 400°F (200°C). Place flour, yeast, and salt in large bowl of standing mixer. Combine olive oil and warm water in measuring cup. Slowly incorporate tablespoons of oil mixture into flour, then change to dough hook attachment and knead for 5 to 6 minutes, until dough is smooth and elastic. Turn dough into lightly oiled bowl, cover with plastic wrap, and place in warm spot to rise for 1 hour, or until doubled in size. Punch dough down once to deflate and turn onto lightly floured board or counter. Using sharp knife, divide dough in half. Using fingers or rolling pin, shape first piece into oblong shape, roughly 10 x 6 in. (25 x 15 cm.). With fingertips, dimple surface of dough, and spread half roasted garlic on each piece. Cover breads with a few overlapping damp paper towels and set aside for 20 minutes. Lightly flour pizza peel. Gently shake hearth breads, one at a time, onto baking stone or tiles. Bake for 20 minutes, until puffy and golden brown. Transfer to wire rack and cool for 20 minutes.

Makes 2. Serves 4–6.

poppy seed flatbread

see variations page 221

This pretty flatbread uses quick-rise yeast, so the combined rising time is less than one hour.

3 cups bread flour
2 cups all-purpose flour
2 tsp. quick-rise yeast
2 tsp. salt
3 tbsp. sugar

3 tbsp. extra-virgin
   olive oil
2 cups warm water
2 tbsp. milk
1/4 cup poppy seeds

In large bowl of standing mixer, combine 2 cups flour, yeast, salt, and sugar. Combine oil and warm water. Pour oil mixture into flour mixture and combine slowly, until flour is moistened. Add remaining flour 1/2 cup at a time. When all flour is incorporated, change to dough hook attachment and knead for 4 to 5 minutes, until dough is smooth and elastic. Cover bowl with plastic wrap and place in warm spot to rise for 30 minutes. Preheat oven to 375°F (190°C). Punch dough down once to deflate. Using sharp knife, cut dough in half.

Roll out each piece into an oblong shape, 1 in. (2.5 cm.) thick. Place each loaf on cookie sheet lined with parchment paper. Dimple surface of dough with fingers, cover with clean dish towels, and set aside for 15 minutes. Press dimples once more, brush top of each loaf with 1 tablespoon milk, and sprinkle 2 tablespoons poppy seeds on top. Bake for 25 to 30 minutes, until puffy and golden brown. Serve warm or at room temperature.

Makes 2. Serves 6–8.

matzoh

see base recipe page 199

matzoh with sesame seeds

Prepare the basic recipe, spreading 1 to 2 cups sesame seeds on a clean board. Once matzoh has been rolled and cut, press both sides of piece into seeds, until each piece is well covered. Shake off excess before baking.

matzoh with poppy seeds

Prepare the basic recipe, spreading 1 to 2 cups poppy seeds on a clean board. Once matzoh has been rolled and cut, press both sides of piece into seeds, until each piece is well covered. Shake off excess before baking.

matzoh with honey

Prepare the basic recipe, spreading 1 tablespoon honey on each piece before serving.

matzoh with halvah

Prepare the basic recipe, topping each piece of matzoh with 1 to 2 slices halvah before serving.

matzoh with tahini

Prepare the basic recipe, spreading each piece with 1 tablespoon tahini before serving.

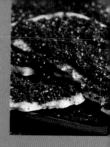

manakish

see base recipe page 200

manakish with feta
Prepare the basic recipe, topping manakish with 1/2 cup crumbled
feta before baking.

manakish with tomato
Prepare the basic recipe, topping manakish with 1 small chopped tomato
before baking.

manakish with fresh mint leaves
Prepare the basic recipe, sprinkling baked manakish with 3 to 4 torn
fresh mint leaves.

manakish with black olives
Prepare the basic recipe, topping manakish with 1/2 cup sliced black
olives before baking.

manakish with pickled turnip
Prepare the basic recipe, topping manakish with 1/2 cup chopped
pickled turnip.

variations

sangak

see base recipe page 203

sangak with poppy seeds
Prepare the basic recipe, replacing the sesame seeds with an equal quantity of poppy seeds.

sangak with nigella seeds
Prepare the basic recipe, replacing the sesame seeds with an equal quantity of nigella seeds.

sangak with cumin seeds
Prepare the basic recipe, replacing the sesame seeds with 2 tablespoons cumin seeds. Sprinkle 1/2 teaspoon over each piece of sangak.

sangak with coriander seeds
Prepare the basic recipe, replacing the sesame seeds with 2 tablespoons coriander seeds. Sprinkle 1/2 teaspoon over each piece of sangak.

sangak with caraway seeds
Prepare the basic recipe, replacing the sesame seeds with 2 tablespoons caraway seeds. Sprinkle 1/2 teaspoon over each piece of sangak.

barbari

see base recipe page 204

barbari with feta
Prepare the basic recipe, topping each barbari with 1/2 cup crumbled
feta before baking.

barbari with nigella seeds
Prepare the basic recipe, replacing the sesame seeds with an equal quantity
of nigella seeds.

barbari with raisins
Prepare the basic recipe, adding 1/3 cup sultana raisins with the flour.

barbari with oats
Prepare the basic recipe, omitting sesame seeds. Sprinkle each barbari with
2 tablespoons quick-cooking oats.

barbari with sunflower seeds
Prepare the basic recipe, replacing sesame seeds with an equal quantity
of sunflower seeds.

variations

pita

see base recipe page 208

garlic pita chips
Preheat oven 350°F (175°C). Cut pita into 6 equal wedges and place on large baking sheet. Coat each wedge with a thin film of extra-virgin olive oil and sprinkle with a pinch of garlic salt. Bake until crisp for 5 to 7 minutes.

pita with hummus
Prepare the basic recipe, topping each pita with 2 tablespoons hummus before serving.

pita with tzatziki
Prepare the basic recipe, topping each pita with 2 tablespoons tzatziki before serving.

whole-wheat pita
Prepare the basic recipe, replacing the all-purpose flour with an equal quantity of whole-wheat flour.

pita with pomegranate & mint yogurt dip
Prepare the basic recipe, topping each pita with a dip made of 1 tablespoon chopped fresh mint, 2 tablespoons natural yogurt, and a pinch of salt. Sprinkle 1 tablespoon pomegranate seeds over the yogurt dip.

lavash

see base recipe page 208

lavash with toasted sesame seeds
Prepare the basic recipe, adding 1/2 teaspoon toasted sesame seeds
to the dough with the flour.

lavash with poppy seeds
Prepare the basic recipe, adding 1 teaspoon poppy seeds to the dough
with the flour.

lavash with sunflower seeds
Prepare the basic recipe, adding 1 teaspoon chopped sunflower seeds
to the dough with the flour.

lavash with cumin seeds
Prepare the basic recipe, adding 1/2 teaspoon slightly crushed cumin
seeds to the dough with the flour.

lavash with ground sumac
Prepare the basic recipe, adding 1/2 teaspoon ground sumac to the dough
with the flour.

variations

garlic hearth bread

see base recipe page 211

garlic & cheese hearth bread
Prepare the basic recipe, sprinkling 1/4 cup finely grated Parmesan
over the roasted garlic mixture.

garlic & thyme hearth bread
Prepare the basic recipe, adding 1/4 teaspoon dried and crumbled thyme
to the roasted garlic mixture.

garlic & rosemary hearth bread
Prepare the basic recipe, adding 1/4 teaspoon dried and crumbled rosemary
to the roasted garlic mixture.

garlic & pink peppercorn hearth bread
Prepare the basic recipe, adding 1 teaspoon ground pink peppercorns
to the dough just before changing to the dough hook attachment.

garlic & parsley hearth bread
Prepare the basic recipe, adding 1/4 cup chopped fresh flat-leaf parsley
to the roasted garlic mixture.

poppy seed flatbread

see base recipe page 212

garlic & poppy seed flatbread
Prepare the basic recipe, sprinkling 1 minced garlic clove over each flatbread with the poppy seeds.

celery & poppy seed flatbread
Prepare the basic recipe, sprinkling 1/4 teaspoon celery seeds over each flatbread with the poppy seeds.

poppy seed flatbread with smoked paprika
Prepare the basic recipe, adding 1/4 teaspoon smoked paprika to the dough just before changing to the dough hook attachment.

poppy seed flatbread with cumin
Prepare the basic recipe, adding 1/4 teaspoon ground cumin to the dough just before changing to the dough hook attachment.

poppy seed flatbread with cardamom
Prepare the basic recipe, adding 1/4 teaspoon ground cardamom to the dough just before changing to the dough hook attachment.

flatbreads of the americas

In the earliest settlements in all regions of the Americas, people have taken grain, ground it, mixed it with water, and cooked it over fire. This chapter contains the best of these enduring recipes.

wheat tortillas

see variations page 242

Used for making everything from burritos to quesadillas and wraps, this is one recipe you'll want to master.

2 cups bread flour, preferably unbleached
1/2 tsp. salt
3 tbsp. corn oil
1/2 cup warm water

In large bowl of standing mixer, combine flour and salt. Slowly stir in oil. When oil is well incorporated, add warm water. Mix on slow speed until all flour is moistened and dough sticks together. Add up to 1/4 cup more water as necessary to get dough to hold. Change to dough hook and knead for 1 to 2 minutes. Turn dough onto lightly floured surface and divide into 8 equal portions. Shape pieces into 3-in (8-cm.) discs, place on cookie sheet, and cover with plastic wrap. Set aside for 30 minutes.

Using a tortilla press or a rolling pin, roll out discs to form 8-in (20-cm.) tortillas. Preheat large cast-iron or nonstick skillet over medium heat.

Place first tortilla in hot skillet and cook for less than 1 minute per side, or until brown spots appear. Repeat with remaining dough. Stack cooked tortillas and keep warm in tortilla basket or wrapped in a clean paper towel.

Makes 8. Serves 3–4.

masa harina tortillas

see variations page 243

In Mexico, corn is soaked in a water and quicklime mixture to soften the grain and help remove the husks before it is ground into flour for corn tortillas. To skip this step, buy prepared masa harina, a flour developed specifically for tortillas.

2 cups masa harina
1 1/4 cups hot water

In large bowl of standing mixer, combine masa harina and hot water. Mix on slow speed until all flour is moistened and dough sticks together. Add more water or flour as necessary to get a soft dough that is not sticky.

Change to dough hook and knead for 1 to 2 minutes. Turn dough onto lightly floured surface and divide into 16 equal portions. Shape each piece into a ball and flatten into a 2-in (5-cm.) disc.

Using a tortilla press or a rolling pin, roll out discs to form 6-in (15-cm.) tortillas. Preheat large cast-iron or nonstick skillet over medium heat.

Place first tortilla in hot skillet and cook for less than 1 minute per side, or until brown spots appear. Repeat with remaining dough. Stack cooked tortillas and keep warm in tortilla basket or wrapped in a clean paper towel.

Makes 16. Serves 6–8.

bannock

see variations page 244

Bannock can be cooked in a cast-iron skillet over a campfire, or even wrapped around a stick and held 8 in. (20 cm.) over flames until cooked.

1 cup all-purpose flour
1 tsp. baking powder
1/4 tbsp. salt
3 tbsp. unsalted butter
1/2 cup water

In large bowl, combine flour, baking powder, and salt. Cut in the butter until the mixture resembles a coarse meal. Add 1/2 cup water and stir until flour is moistened and a stiff dough forms. Add more water if necessary.

Lightly oil and preheat large cast-iron or nonstick skillet over medium heat.

Turn dough onto lightly floured board or counter. Divide into 4 equal pieces. Flatten each piece to form a disc 1/2 in. (1 cm.) thick.

Place first disc in hot skillet and cook for 6 to 7 minutes per side. Serve warm with butter or desired topping.

Makes 4. Serves 2–4.

pan fry bread

see variations page 245

This deep-fried Navajo bread is often served at powwows and First Nations gatherings around North America.

3 cups unbleached all-purpose flour
1 tbsp. baking powder
1/8 tsp. baking soda
1 tsp. salt

3/4 cup whole milk
3/4 cup hot water
1 tbsp. canola oil, plus more for
    deep-frying

In large bowl of standing mixer, combine flour, baking powder, baking soda, and salt. Combine milk and hot water and stir into flour mixture.

Change to dough hook attachment and knead for 2 to 3 minutes, until you have a smooth dough. Turn dough into oiled bowl, rolling dough so it is covered in a light oil film. Cover bowl with plastic wrap and set aside for 30 minutes.

Turn dough onto lightly floured board or counter. Divide dough into 10 equal pieces. Shape pieces into balls and flatten each ball to form a disc, 5 in. (12 cm.) wide and 1/8 in. (0.5 cm.) thick.

Deep-fry pieces of dough in 2 in. (5 cm.) hot oil for 1 minute per side, until golden brown. Transfer fry bread to paper towel to drain. Serve warm.

Makes 10. Serves 4–5.

gorditas

see variations page 246

Gorditas are the stuffed flatbreads popular in the Durango region of Mexico. The name accurately translates into "little fat ones!"

1 cup masa harina
1 1/2 tsp. salt
1/2 tsp. baking powder
2 tbsp. all-purpose flour
1 cup warm water
1/2 lb. lean ground beef

1/2 yellow onion, finely chopped
freshly ground black pepper
pinch of chili powder
1 1/2 cups grated Monterey
  Jack cheese
canola oil for deep-frying

In large bowl of standing mixer, combine masa harina, 1/2 teaspoon salt, baking powder, and flour. Add warm water and mix on slow speed until all flour is moistened and dough sticks together. Add more water or flour as necessary to get a soft dough that is not sticky. Change to dough hook and knead for 1 to 2 minutes. Cover bowl with plastic wrap and set aside for 30 minutes. To prepare filling, brown the beef and onions over medium heat in a large, cast-iron skillet until meat is cooked through and onions have softened and are beginning to brown, 4 to 5 minutes. Stir in remaining ingredients except cheese and set aside. Preheat oven to 350°F (175°C). Turn dough onto lightly floured surface. Divide dough into 6 equal pieces. Roll pieces into balls, then flatten each into a 2 1/2-in (6-cm.) disc, 1/4 in. (0.5 cm.) thick. Working with one piece at a time and keeping the remaining pieces covered to prevent drying, deep-fry discs in 2 in. (5 cm.) hot oil for less than 1 minute per side, carefully

spooning hot oil over the top, until puffy and golden brown. Using tongs, transfer to paper towel to drain. Use a sharp bread knife to slice gordita in half horizontally. Spread 1/3 cup filling over bottom half, cover and sprinkle with 1/4 cup grated cheese. Place stuffed gordita on ovenproof plate and place in preheated oven to keep warm. Repeat with remaining pieces.

Makes 6. Serves 2–3.

arepas

see variations page 247

Arepas are a Venezuelan specialty, common at food stalls and cooked at home.
Eat them plain, as an alternative to bread rolls, or fill them and serve as a sandwich.

2 cups masa harina
1/2 tsp. salt
2 1/3 cups warm water
2 tbsp. canola oil

Preheat oven to 400°F (200°C). In large bowl of standing mixer, combine masa harina and salt. Add hot water and mix on slow speed until all flour is moistened and dough sticks together. Let sit for 5 minutes.

Change to dough hook and knead for 1 to 2 minutes. Turn dough onto lightly floured surface. Divide dough into 8 equal pieces. Roll pieces into balls, then flatten into 3-in (8-cm.) discs, 3/4 in. (2 cm.) thick. Preheat oil in large skillet.

Working with one or two pieces at a time and keeping the remaining pieces covered to prevent drying, fry discs for 3 to 4 minute per side, flipping 3 to 4 times, until crisp and golden brown. Transfer arepas to paper towel to drain. Repeat with remaining pieces.

Place fried arepas on cookie sheet and bake in preheated oven for 15 minutes. Serve warm or at room temperature.

Makes 8. Serves 3–4.

jamaican bammy bread

see variations page 248

This Jamaican specialty is soaked in coconut milk before being fried a second time.
It is traditionally enjoyed with fried fish.

1 lb. cassava (yucca), approx. 2 large
pinch of salt
3 tbsp. unsalted butter
1 cup coconut milk

Peel and finely grate cassava. Press through clean paper towel to remove as much moisture
as possible. Add salt and divide into three 1-cup portions.

Flatten portion to form a disc 6 in. (15 cm.) in diameter and 1/2 in. (1 cm.) thick. Heat
1 tablespoon butter in skillet. Once butter has melted, place first disc in skillet and cook over
medium heat for 9 to 10 minutes. Flip bammy and cook on other side for 9 to 10 minutes.

Remove bammy and place in shallow dish with coconut milk to soak for 5 to 10 minutes.

Return bammy to skillet and cook over medium heat for 3 to 4 minutes per side, until each
side is golden brown. Repeat with 2 other discs.

Makes 3.

cornbread

see variations page 249

Cornbread is a popular bread enjoyed all over the Americas. It is easy to make and satisfying with chili or other spicy stews.

3 tbsp. vegetable shortening (bacon drippings
    can be substituted)
2 large eggs
1 1/2 cups cornmeal

1 tsp. salt
1/2 tsp. baking soda
1 1/4 cups buttermilk

Preheat oven to 400°F (200°C). If baking cornbread in 10-in (25-cm.) cast-iron skillet, heat shortening in skillet. Otherwise, melt shortening and place in a large rectangular baking dish, 9 x 13 in. (23 x 33 cm.).

Place eggs in large bowl of standing mixer. Beat on medium-high speed until frothy. Stir in cornmeal, salt, and baking soda until well incorporated. Stir in buttermilk until mixture is smooth.

Tilt skillet to make sure surface is completely covered in shortening, then pour remaining shortening into the batter. Stir to blend.

Pour batter in skillet and bake 25 to 30 minutes, until cornbread is firm and pulling away from sides of skillet. Slice into wedges and serve hot.

Makes 1. Serves 6–8.

sope

see variations page 250

Sope is a Mexican corn patty that can be topped with any number of savory fillings.

3 cups masa harina
1 cup canned or frozen corn
1/2 cup vegetable shortening

3 tbsp. water
1/4 tsp. salt
freshly ground white pepper

In large bowl of standing mixer, combine masa harina, corn, shortening, water, and salt. Mix with paddle attachment until dough comes together. Add more water if necessary for dough to hold.

Change to dough hook attachment and knead for 3 to 4 minutes, until dough is smooth. Turn dough onto lightly floured board or counter. Using lightly floured rolling pin, roll dough out to 1 in. (2 cm.) thickness. Cut rounds with 4-in. (10-cm.) cookie cutter.

Preheat large cast-iron or nonstick skillet over medium heat. Cook sopes one at a time for 3 minutes per side.

Transfer to paper towel to drain. Season with white pepper.

Repeat until all sopes are cooked. If serving warm, place sopes on lightly greased baking sheet and place in preheated 275°F (140°C) oven until ready to serve.

Makes 12. Serves 6–8.

pupusa

see variations page 251

Pupusas are stuffed corn flatbreads that originate from El Salvador, where they are served with hot sauce and curtido, a condiment similar to coleslaw.

5 cups masa harina
4 cups water
14-oz. can refried beans
3 cups shredded mozzarella
extra-virgin olive oil

In large bowl of standing mixer, combine masa harina and water until all flour is incorporated and a dough forms. Turn onto lightly floured board or counter and divide dough into 25 equal pieces. Roll each piece into a ball and flatten into a 1/2-in thick (1-cm.) disc. Place 1 tablespoon refried beans and 2 tablespoons shredded mozzarella in the middle of the disc, fold over, and flatten once more so that filling is completely covered in dough.

Brush large cast-iron or nonstick skillet with extra-virgin olive oil and preheat over medium heat. Cook pupusas one at a time for 4 to 5 minutes per side, until firm and golden brown. Transfer to paper towel to drain. Repeat until all pupusas are cooked.

Place cooked pupusas on lightly greased baking sheet and keep warm in preheated 275°F (140°C) oven until ready to serve.

Makes 25. Serves 8–10.

variations

wheat tortillas

see base recipe page 223

herb tortillas
Prepare the basic recipe, adding 1/2 teaspoon Italian seasoning.

sun-dried tomato tortillas
Prepare the basic recipe, adding a 1 5/8 oz. package of sun-dried tomato pesto mix to the flour mixture.

whole-wheat tortillas
Prepare the basic recipe, replacing 1 cup bread flour with 1 cup whole-wheat flour.

wheat tortilla chips
Prepare the basic recipe. Once the tortillas have completely cooled, cut each tortilla in half, and each half in fourths, so that you have 8 equal wedges. Preheat oven to 350°F (175°C). Place tortilla wedges in single layer on large baking sheet and bake for 10 to 12 minutes, until golden brown.

spicy tortilla chips
Prepare the basic recipe. Once the tortillas have completely cooled, cut each tortilla into 8 equal wedges. Preheat oven to 350°F (175°C). Place wedges in single layer on baking sheet, brush with olive oil, and sprinkle with a pinch of BBQ or Cajun seasoning. Bake for 10 to 12 minutes, until golden brown.

variations

masa harina tortillas

see base recipe page 224

masa harina tortilla chips
Prepare the basic recipe. Once the tortillas have completely cooled, cut each tortilla in half, and each half in fourths, so that you have 8 equal wedges. Preheat oven to 350°F (175°C). Place tortilla wedges in single layer on large baking sheet, and bake for 10 to 12 minutes, until golden brown.

masa harina tortillas with chili pepper
Prepare the basic recipe, adding a pinch of crushed red pepper flakes to the masa harina mixture.

masa harina tortillas with mixed peppercorns
Prepare the basic recipe, adding 1/4 teaspoon freshly ground mixed peppercorns to the masa harina mixture.

blue corn tortillas
Prepare the basic recipe, replacing the masa harina with 1 cup blue cornmeal and 1 cup all-purpose flour.

variations

bannock

see base recipe page 227

bannock with blueberries
Prepare the basic recipe, folding 1/4 cup fresh blueberries into the dough.

bannock with raisins
Prepare the basic recipe, folding 1/4 cup raisins into the dough.

bannock with cranberries
Prepare the basic recipe, folding 1/4 cup fresh or frozen cranberries
into the dough.

cinnamon bannock
Prepare the basic recipe, adding 1/4 teaspoon ground cinnamon
with the flour.

variations

pan fry bread

see base recipe page 228

pan fry bread with wild blueberry jam
Prepare the basic recipe, topping each fry bread with 2 tablespoons
wild blueberry jam before serving.

pan fry bread with maple syrup
Prepare the basic recipe, drizzling 1 tablespoon maple syrup over each
piece of fry bread before serving.

pan fry bread with fresh tomato salsa
Prepare the basic recipe, topping each fry bread with 2 tablespoons
fresh tomato salsa before serving.

pan fry bread with sugar & lemon juice
Prepare the basic recipe, topping each piece of fry bread with 1 teaspoon
granulated sugar and 1/2 teaspoon fresh lemon juice before serving.

variations

gorditas

see base recipe page 230

whole-wheat gorditas
Prepare the basic recipe, replacing 1/2 cup masa harina with 1/2 cup whole-wheat flour.

gorditas stuffed with prickly pear
Prepare the basic recipe, replacing the beef filling with 1/4 cup prickly pear (*nopales*) salsa.

gorditas with chicken
Prepare the basic recipe, replacing the beef filling with 1/4 cup shredded cooked chicken and 1 tablespoon tomato salsa.

gorditas with green salsa
Prepare the basic recipe, adding 1 tablespoon green salsa to teach gordita with the beef filling.

variations

arepas

see base recipe page 233

blue corn flour arepas
Prepare the basic recipe, replacing the masa harina with 1 cup blue cornmeal
and 1 cup all-purpose flour.

arepas stuffed with scrambled egg
Prepare the basic recipe, slicing each arepa in half horizontally and filling
with 2 to 3 tablespoons scrambled eggs.

whole-wheat arepas
Prepare the basic recipe, replacing 1 cup masa harina with 1 cup whole-
wheat flour.

coconut arepas
Prepare the basic recipe, adding 1/4 cup shredded coconut to the masa
harina mixture.

variations

jamaican bammy bread

see base recipe page 234

potato bammy bread
Prepare the basic recipe, replacing 1 cup grated cassava with 1 cup finely grated potato.

sweet potato bammy bread
Prepare the basic recipe, replacing 1 cup grated cassava with 1 cup finely grated sweet potato.

beet & cassava bammy bread
Prepare the basic recipe, replacing 1 cup grated cassava with 1 cup finely grated beet.

carrot & cassava bammy bread
Prepare the basic recipe, replacing 1 cup grated cassava with 1 cup finely grated carrot.

variations

cornbread

see base recipe page 237

cornbread with cayenne pepper
Prepare the basic recipe, adding a pinch of cayenne pepper with
the cornmeal.

cornbread with sweet red pepper
Prepare the basic recipe, adding 1/2 large red bell pepper, diced, with
the cornmeal.

corn & cheese bread
Prepare the basic recipe, adding 1/3 cup grated cheddar or Monterey Jack
cheese to the batter with the cornmeal. Sprinkle 1/4 cup grated cheese
on top of batter before baking.

cornbread with dill
Prepare the basic recipe, adding 1 tsp. dried or 1 tbsp. chopped fresh
dill to the batter with the cornmeal.

variations

sope

see base recipe page 238

sope with chili pepper
Prepare the basic recipe, adding 1/2 teaspoon crushed red pepper flakes to the dough with the masa harina.

sope with guacamole
Prepare the basic recipe, topping each sope with 1/4 cup guacamole and 2 to 3 leaves fresh cilantro before serving.

sope with shredded pork
Prepare the basic recipe, topping each sope with 1/4 cup shredded cooked pork and 2 tablespoons tomato salsa before serving.

sope with green olives
Prepare the basic recipe, topping each sope with 2 tablespoons sliced green olives before serving.

sope with chicken
Prepare the basic recipe, topping each sope with 1/4 cup shredded cooked chicken and 2 tablespoons tomato salsa before serving.

variations

pupusa

see base recipe page 241

rice pupusa
Prepare the basic recipe, replacing 1 cup masa harina with 1 cup rice flour.

pupusa filled with chicharron
Prepare the basic recipe, replacing the refried bean filling with chicharron. To prepare the chicharron, slice 1 lb. pork skin into 2-in. (5-cm.) slices and sprinkle with salt. Cover and place in refrigerator for 1 hour. Fry pork slices for 5 to 6 minutes, until crispy. Drain on paper towels.

pupusa filled with green salsa
Prepare the basic recipe, topping each pupusa with 1 tablespoon green salsa.

pupusa stuffed with cheese and herbs
Prepare the basic recipe, omitting refried beans. Add 1 tablespoon finely chopped fresh cilantro to each pupusa with the shredded mozzarella.

sweet pizzas & flatbreads

When you are craving something sweet

and a little different, try one of these

scrumptious treats.

chocolate pizza

see variations page 272

This dessert is easy to assemble and always a big hit with chocolate lovers.

1/3 recipe basic thin pizza crust
   (page 17)
2 tsp. unsalted butter, melted

1/3 cup prepared chocolate sauce
1/4 cup white chocolate chips
1/4 cup milk chocolate chips

Place pizza stone on bottom rack of oven and preheat to 450°F (230°C). Roll pizza dough out to a 10-in. (25-cm.) round.

Lightly flour pizza peel. Place pizza crust on peel, dimple surface with fingertips, and glaze with unsalted butter. Gently shake pizza from peel onto baking stone.

Bake for 15 to 20 minutes, until crust is slightly puffy and golden brown.

Remove crust from oven. Spread chocolate sauce over pizza crust, sprinkle chocolate chips over the sauce, then return to oven for 1 to 2 minutes, until chocolate chips begin to melt.

Transfer to wire rack to cool. Serve warm or at room temperature.

Makes one 10-in. (25-cm.) pizza. Serves 4–6.

apple cranberry pizza

see variations page 273

It is not surprising to find that fruit makes a tempting topping for pizzas!

1/3 recipe basic thin pizza crust (page 17)
1/3 cup dried cranberries
4 medium apples, peeled, cored, and finely
   chopped

3 tbsp. brown sugar
2 tbsp. unsalted butter, melted
1–2 tsp. freshly squeezed lemon juice
1 tsp. ground cinnamon

Place pizza stone on middle rack of oven and preheat to 450°F (230°C). Roll pizza dough out to a 12-in. (30-cm.) round. Lightly flour pizza peel.

Place pizza crust on peel, and sprinkle with dried cranberries. In medium bowl, combine chopped apple, sugar, butter, lemon juice, and cinnamon.

Spread apple mixture over cranberries. Gently shake pizza from peel onto baking stone.

Bake for 15 to 20 minutes, until crust is slightly puffy and golden brown.

Remove crust from oven and transfer to wire rack to cool. Serve warm or at room temperature.

Makes one 12-in. (30-cm.) pizza. Serves 4–6.

streusel pizza

see variations page 274

This luscious pizza is topped with a cream cheese mixture, fresh berries, and a crumbly topping.

1/3 recipe basic thin pizza crust (page 17)
topping
1/2 cup cream cheese, softened
1 large egg yolk
1/4 tsp. vanilla extract
1 1/2 tsp. sugar
1/2 cup fresh strawberries, hulled

streusel
1/3 cup light brown sugar
2 tbsp. unsalted butter, melted
1 tbsp. all-purpose flour

Preheat oven to 400°F (200°C).

Line a 12-in. (30-cm.) pizza pan with parchment paper. Roll pizza dough out to a 12-in. (30-cm.) round and place in pan. In medium bowl, combine cream cheese, egg yolk, vanilla, and sugar. Stir until smooth.

In small bowl, combine all the streusel ingredients until you have a crumbly mixture. Spread the cream cheese mixture over the pizza crust, top with strawberries, and sprinkle with streusel.

Place on middle rack of preheated oven and bake for 25 to 30 minutes, until crust is baked and streusel is crunchy. Serve warm or at room temperature.

Makes one 12-in. (30-cm.) pizza. Serves 4–6.

vanilla flatbread

see variations page 275

This gently scented flatbread pairs perfectly with a cup of tea or a café au lait.

dough
2 1/2 tsp. active dry yeast
1/2 tsp. sugar
1/2 cup warm water
1/3 cup all-purpose flour
1/3 cup whole milk
1/4 cup sugar
pinch of salt

4 tsp. vanilla extract
1 vanilla bean, seeds
   scraped
3 large eggs
2 1/4 cups all-purpose flour
1/2 cup unsalted butter,
   softened and cut into
   8 pieces

glaze
3 tbsp. unsalted butter,
   melted
1 tsp. vanilla extract
1/4 cup raw sugar

To prepare the dough, sprinkle yeast and 1/2 teaspoon sugar over warm water in medium bowl. Set aside for 5 minutes, until foamy. Add 1/3 cup flour and stir until mixture is smooth. Cover with plastic wrap and set aside for 30 minutes. Slowly heat milk in medium saucepan over low heat. Stir in 1/4 cup sugar and salt. Remove from heat and cool for 2 to 3 minutes. Pour milk mixture into large bowl of standing mixer. Add vanilla extract, seeds, and eggs and mix on slow speed until well blended. Blend in yeast mixture, then add flour 3/4 cup at a time. Add butter, one piece at a time. Change to dough hook and knead for 4 to 5 minutes until dough is smooth, elastic, and sticky. Turn dough into lightly greased bowl, cover with plastic wrap, and place in a warm spot to rise for 1 1/2 to 2 hours, until doubled in size. Cover 2 large rectangular cookie sheets with parchment paper. Turn dough onto lightly floured surface. Using a sharp knife, cut dough in half. Shape each piece into an oblong,

roughly 8–9 in. (20-23 cm.) long shape. Place on cookie sheets, cover with a clean paper towel, and return to warm spot to rise for 1 additional hour. Preheat oven to 375°F (190°C). To prepare the glaze, combine melted butter and vanilla. Glaze the surfaces of both flatbreads, then sprinkle each with 2 tablespoons raw sugar. Bake flatbreads for 25 minutes, until tops are golden brown. Transfer to wire rack to cool. Serve warm or at room temperature.

Makes 2. Serves 6–8.

sweet fried flatbread

see variations page 276

Similar in taste and texture to sugar doughnuts, this cinnamon-dusted fried flatbread is sure to please.

1/3 cup sugar
1/2 cup warm water
5 tsp. active dry yeast
pinch of sugar
1 cup warm milk
1 tsp. vanilla extract
2 large eggs

1/3 cup canola oil
4 1/4–5 cups all-purpose flour
1 1/2 tsp. salt
canola oil for frying

topping
1 cup sugar

In large bowl of standing mixer, sprinkle yeast and pinch of sugar over warm water. Set aside for 5 minutes, until yeast becomes foamy. With paddle attachment, stir in remaining sugar, milk, vanilla, eggs, and oil. Stir in 4 cups of flour and the salt. Add more flour as necessary to form a soft dough. With dough hook, knead for 4 to 5 minutes, until dough is smooth and elastic. Cover bowl with plastic wrap and set aside for 1 hour. Turn dough onto lightly floured board to deflate. Using sharp knife, divide dough into 22 to 24 equal egg-sized pieces. Shape each piece into a ball. Using rolling pin or fingers, stretch out each ball to form a 6-in. (15-cm.) oval, 1/8 in. (0.5 cm.) thick. Keep rolled-out pieces covered while you prepare the remaining ones. Deep-fry pieces of dough in 2 in. (5 cm.) hot oil for 1 minute per side, until dark golden brown. Remove with tongs and transfer to paper towels to drain. Place sugar in a large bowl. Toss flatbread in sugar, shaking off excess as you pull them out of the bowl. Serve warm.

Makes 22–24. Serves 10–12.

lemon & cranberry flatbread

see variations page 277

This is a wonderfully fun and deliciously tart flatbread.

2 1/2 tsp. active dry yeast
1/2 tsp. sugar
1/2 cup warm water
1/3 cup all-purpose flour
1/3 cup whole milk
1/4 cup sugar
pinch of salt

3 large eggs
2 1/4 cups all-purpose flour
1/2 cup unsalted butter, softened and
    cut into 8 pieces
juice and zest of 1 large lemon
1/3 cup dried cranberries

To prepare dough, sprinkle yeast and 1/2 teaspoon sugar over warm water in medium bowl.
Set aside for 5 minutes, until foamy. Add 1/3 cup flour and stir until smooth. Cover with plastic
wrap and set aside for 30 minutes. Heat milk in medium saucepan over low heat. Stir in 1/4 cup
sugar and salt. Remove from heat and cool for 2 to 3 minutes. Pour milk mixture into large bowl
of standing mixer. Add eggs and mix on slow speed until blended. Stir in yeast mixture, then add
flour 3/4 cup at a time. Add butter, one piece at a time. Stir in lemon zest, juice, and cranberries.
Change to dough hook and knead for 4 to 5 minutes until dough is smooth, elastic, and sticky.
Turn dough into lightly greased bowl, cover with plastic wrap, and place in warm spot to rise for
1 1/2 to 2 hours, until doubled in size. Cover 2 large rectangular cookie sheets with parchment
paper. Turn dough onto lightly floured surface. Using sharp knife, cut dough in half. Shape each
piece into an oblong, roughly 8-9 in. (20-23 cm.) long. Place on cookie sheets, cover with paper
towel, and return to warm spot to rise for 1 additional hour. Preheat oven to 375°F (190°C)
and bake flatbreads for 25 minutes, until tops are golden brown. Transfer to wire rack to cool.

Makes 2. Serves 6-8.

ice cream pizza with brownie crust

see variations page 278

The ultimate way to reward someone who has earned a lot of brownie points!

crust
1/2 cup all-purpose flour
1/2 tsp. baking powder
1/2 tsp. salt
1/4 cup unsalted butter

3 oz. unsweetened chocolate,
   roughly chopped
1 cup sugar
2 large eggs, lightly beaten
1 tsp. vanilla extract

toppings
1 cup whipping cream
1 tbsp. confectioners' sugar
2 cups vanilla ice cream
1/3 cup assorted candies
   for decoration

Preheat oven to 350°F (175°C). Line a 12-in. (30-cm.) x 1/2-in. (1-cm.) pizza pan with parchment paper. In a small bowl, combine flour, baking powder, and salt. In a double boiler, melt butter and chocolate until smooth. Remove from heat. Stir in sugar, eggs, and vanilla. Add flour mixture and stir until just combined. Spread brownie batter over parchment paper in pizza pan. Bake on middle rack in oven for 13 to 15 minutes, until surface does not keep indentation when touched. Transfer to wire rack and cool to room temperature. Transfer pan to refrigerator to cool for 30 minutes. Using standing mixer, beat whipping cream and confectioners' sugar until stiff peaks form. Remove ice cream from freezer 5 minutes before you take the crust out of the refrigerator. Spread the softened ice cream in a 1/2-in. (1-cm.) layer over the brownie layer, leaving a 1/4-in. (0.5-cm.) border. Decorate with dollops of whipped cream and candies. Transfer pizza to freezer until ready to serve.

Makes one 12-in. (30-cm.) pizza. Serves 4–6.

chocolate chip cookie crust pizza

see variations page 279

If you ever have a group of children you really want to impress, try out this decadent dessert.

crust
2 cups all-purpose flour
1 tsp. baking soda
1/2 tsp. salt
3/4 cup unsalted butter,
    softened

1 1/4 cup light brown sugar
1 large egg, lightly beaten
2 tsp. vanilla extract
1 1/2 cups semisweet
    chocolate chips

topping
1 1/2 cups prepared
    marshmallow topping
1/3 cup prepared butterscotch
    sauce

Preheat oven to 350°F (175°C). In medium bowl, combine flour, baking soda, and salt. Set aside.

In large bowl of standing mixer, beat butter and brown sugar for 2 minutes, or until light and fluffy. Stir in egg and vanilla until well blended. Add flour mixture and stir just until it is incorporated. Stir in chocolate chips.

Line a 12-in. (30-cm.) pizza pan with parchment paper. Turn dough onto pan and press down until pan is covered and top is smooth. Bake for 30 to 35 minutes, until top is golden brown and edges are a deeper brown. Transfer to wire rack to cool. Spread marshmallow topping over crust and drizzle with butterscotch sauce.

Makes one 12-in. (30-cm.) pizza. Serves 6–8.

raspberry almond pizza

see variations page 280

This mouthwatering creation features a spectacular blend of marzipan and meringue in the topping.

2/3 recipe basic thin pizza crust (page 17)
3 large egg whites
1/2 cup marzipan, softened
1 cup seedless raspberry jam

1 1/2 cups fresh raspberries
1 1/2 cups slivered almonds,
   toasted
2 tbsp. confectioners' sugar

Preheat oven to 400°F (210°C). Line two 12-in. (30-cm.) pizza pans with parchment paper. Roll pizza dough out to two 12-in. (30-cm.) round discs and place in pans.

In large bowl of standing mixer, beat egg whites until foamy. Add marzipan and stir until smooth. Fold in raspberry jam until fully incorporated.

Spread half the marzipan mixture over each pizza crust, leaving a 1/2-in. (1-cm.) border.

Place on middle rack of preheated oven and bake for 10–12 minutes, until crust is golden brown and topping is firm. Transfer to wire rack to cool.

Sprinkle each pizza with 3/4 cup raspberries, 3/4 cup toasted almonds, and 1 tablespoon confectioners' sugar. Serve immediately.

Makes two 12-in. (30-cm.) pizzas. Serves 10–12.

fig, ricotta & honey pizza

see variations page 281

This delightful breakfast combination makes an elegant dessert pizza.

2/3 recipe basic thin pizza crust (page 17)
1/2 cup ricotta
2 tbsp. confectioners' sugar

4–6 ripe figs, sliced
   lengthwise
3 tbsp. honey

Place pizza stone on middle rack of oven and preheat to 450°F (230°C). Roll pizza dough out to two 12-in. (30-cm.) rounds. Lightly flour pizza peel. Place first pizza crust on peel.

In large bowl of standing mixer, combine ricotta and sugar until smooth. Spread half the ricotta mixture over each pizza crust, leaving a 1/2-in. (1-cm.) border. Arrange half the fig slices and drizzle half the honey on the pizza. Gently shake pizza from peel onto baking stone.

Bake for 12 to 15 minutes, until crust is slightly puffy and golden brown.

Remove pizza from oven and transfer to wire rack to cool. Repeat with second pizza.

Makes two 12-in. (30-cm.) pizzas. Serves 10–12.

variations

chocolate pizza

see base recipe page 253

chocolate hazelnut pizza
Prepare the basic recipe, replacing the prepared chocolate sauce with
an equal quantity of prepared chocolate-hazelnut spread.

chocolate raspberry pizza
Prepare the basic recipe, adding 1/4 cup fresh raspberries over melted
chocolate chips once the pizza has been removed from the oven for
the second time.

chocolate orange pizza
Prepare the basic recipe, replacing the milk chocolate chips with
an equal quantity of chopped orange-flavored chocolate.

chocolate ginger pizza
Prepare the basic recipe, adding 2 tablespoons chopped candied ginger
over melted chocolate chips once the pizza has been removed from the
oven for the second time.

variations

apple cranberry pizza

see base recipe page 254

apple cranberry pizza with coconut
Prepare the basic recipe, adding 1/4 cup shredded coconut to the
apple mixture.

apple cranberry pizza with almonds
Prepare the basic recipe, sprinkling 1/4 cup slivered almonds over
the apple mixture.

apple raisin pizza
Prepare the basic recipe, replacing the dried cranberries with an equal
quantity of raisins.

cardamom apple pizza
Prepare the basic recipe, adding 1/4 teaspoon ground cardamom
to the apple mixture.

variations

streusel pizza

see base recipe page 257

ricotta streusel pizza
Prepare the basic recipe, replacing the cream cheese with an equal quantity of ricotta.

marscapone streusel pizza
Prepare the basic recipe, replacing the cream cheese with an equal quantity of mascarpone.

streusel pizza with raspberries
Prepare the basic recipe, replacing the strawberries with an equal quantity of fresh raspberries.

streusel pizza with mixed berries
Prepare the basic recipe, replacing the strawberries with an equal quantity of assorted fresh berries.

variations

vanilla flatbread

see base recipe page 258

cinnamon flatbread
Prepare the basic recipe, replacing the vanilla extract and seeds with
1/2 teaspoon ground cinnamon. Replace vanilla extract in glaze
with 1/4 teaspoon ground cinnamon.

vanilla cranberry flatbread
Prepare the basic recipe, adding 1/2 cup dried cranberries to the dough
once all the flour has been incorporated.

carob flatbread
Prepare the basic recipe, omitting vanilla extract and seeds and adding
1/4 cup carob powder with the flour. Omit vanilla glaze.

chocolate chip flatbread
Prepare the basic recipe, adding 1/2 cup semisweet chocolate chips
to the dough once all the flour has been incorporated.

variations

sweet fried flatbread

see base recipe page 261

sweet fried flatbread with cinnamon sugar
Prepare the basic recipe, adding 1/2 teaspoon ground cinnamon
to the sugar topping.

sweet fried flatbread with apple compote
Prepare the basic recipe, topping each piece with 2 tablespoons prepared
apple compote.

sweet fried flatbread with chocolate hazelnut spread
Prepare the basic recipe, omitting sugar topping. Top each piece with
2 tablespoons chocolate hazelnut spread.

sweet fried flatbread with candied pecans
Prepare the basic recipe, adding 1/3 cup finely chopped candied pecans
to the dough once the flour has been fully incorporated.

lemon & cranberry flatbread

see base recipe page 262

lemon & blueberry flatbread
Prepare the basic recipe, replacing the dried cranberries with an equal amount of dried blueberries.

lemon & currant flatbread
Prepare the basic recipe, replacing the dried cranberries with an equal quantity of dried currants.

lemon & cherry flatbread
Prepare the basic recipe, replacing the dried cranberries with an equal quantity of dried cherries.

lemon & papaya flatbread
Prepare the basic recipe, replacing the dried cranberries with an equal quantity of dried chopped papaya.

variations

ice cream pizza with brownie crust

see base recipe page 265

chocolate ice cream pizza
Prepare the basic recipe, replacing the vanilla ice cream with an equal quantity of chocolate ice cream.

ice cream pizza with marshmallow topping
Prepare the basic recipe, replacing the whipped cream topping with an equal quantity of marshmallow topping.

rocky road ice cream pizza
Prepare the basic recipe, adding 1/4 cup chopped walnuts to the brownie mixture once the flour has been incorporated. Replace the vanilla ice cream with an equal quantity of rocky road ice cream. Replace assorted candies with 1/4 cup chopped walnuts.

ice cream pizza with butterscotch sauce
Prepare the basic recipe, drizzling 1/3 cup prepared butterscotch sauce over the layer of ice cream before adding the whipped cream and candies.

chocolate chip cookie crust pizza

see base recipe page 266

butterscotch chip cookie crust
Prepare the basic recipe, replacing the semisweet chocolate chips
with an equal quantity of butterscotch chips.

double chocolate cookie crust pizza
Prepare the basic recipe, using a blend of semisweet and milk
chocolate chips.

peanut butter chip cookie crust pizza
Prepare the basic recipe, replacing the chocolate chips with
an equal quantity of peanut butter-flavored chips.

toffee chip cookie crust pizza
Prepare the basic recipe, replacing the chocolate chips with an equal
quantity of toffee chips.

variations

raspberry almond pizza

see base recipe page 269

raspberry almond pizza with chocolate drizzle
Prepare the basic recipe, drizzling each pizza with 1/4 cup melted semisweet chocolate chips after raspberries and sliced almonds have been arranged.

raspberry almond pizza with cookie crust
Prepare the basic recipe, replacing the thin pizza crust with 1 package prepared sugar cookie dough. Roll cookie dough out to form two 12-in. (30-cm.) pizzas, using scraps of dough from first pizza to help make the second. Adjust oven temperature according to package baking instructions.

blackberry almond pizza
Prepare the basic recipe, replacing the seedless raspberry jam with an equal quantity of seedless blackberry jam and the fresh raspberries with an equal quantity of fresh blackberries.

variations

fig, ricotta & honey pizza

see base recipe page 270

fig, ricotta & honey pizza with thyme
Prepare the basic recipe, sprinkling 1/4 teaspoon dried thyme over
the layer of ricotta.

fig, ricotta & maple syrup pizza
Prepare the basic recipe, replacing the honey with an equal quantity
of maple syrup.

fig, mascarpone & honey pizza
Prepare the basic recipe, replacing the ricotta with an equal
quantity of mascarpone.

strawberry, ricotta & balsamic pizza
Prepare the basic recipe, replacing the fig slices with 1/3 cup hulled
strawberries per pizza. Replace the honey with 2 teaspoon balsamic
vinegar per pizza.

index